The Role of Land Reform in Economic Development

PRAEGER SPECIAL STUDIES IN
INTERNATIONAL ECONOMICS AND DEVELOPMENT

The Role of Land Reform in Economic Development

A CASE STUDY OF TAIWAN

Anthony Y. C. Koo

FREDERICK A. PRAEGER, Publishers
New York • Washington • London

The purpose of the Praeger Special Studies is to make specialized research monographs in U.S. and international economics and politics
available to the academic, business, and government communities. For
further information, write to the Special Projects Division, Frederick
A. Praeger, Publishers, 111 Fourth Avenue, New York, N.Y. 10003.

FREDERICK A. PRAEGER, PUBLISHERS
111 Fourth Avenue, New York, N.Y. 10003, U.S.A.
5, Cromwell Place, London S.W.7, England

Published in the United States of America in 1968
by Frederick A. Praeger, Inc., Publishers

Library of Congress Catalog Card Number: 67-29434

Printed in the United States of America

Dedicated to the Memory of
My Parents

ACKNOWLEDGMENTS

Most of the material used in this study was gathered when I was in Taiwan during the 1962-63 academic year, researching under a Ford Foundation grant administered by Michigan State University. I am grateful to the Social Science Research Council for their research grant in 1964 to complete the project.

My friends and associates in Taiwan were most helpful and made my stay a pleasant experience. Unfortunately, it is impossible to list all of them; they know they have my thanks. T. H. Lee patiently worked with me on the details of the data collected by the Sino-American Joint Commission of Rural Reconstruction (JCRR). My research assistant, C. M. Cheng, was both enthusiastic and painstaking in carrying out his assignments. I am indebted to Professor Simon Kuznets for his guidance in structuring the study in the beginning stages of my writing and to Professors Alexander Eckstein and T. C. Liu for reviewing the final manuscript. Professors M. Bronfenbrenner, J. B. Buck, J. B. Hendry, Y. M. Ho, C. H. C. Kao, J. C. Liu, R. C. Porter, W. G. Shepherd, J. Y. Takeshita, L. W. Witt, and K. T. Wright are also thanked for their comments on the manuscript. The opinions expressed in this volume, nevertheless, remain the sole responsibility of the author.

CONTENTS

Chapter   Page

LIST OF TABLES

LIST OF FIGURES

GLOSSARY

chia	0.9699 hectare, or 2.3968 acres.
grades of land	Superior quality (1st to 8th grades); Medium quality (9th to 18th grades); Inferior quality (19th to 26th grades).
hsien	County.
n.a.	Indicates no figures available.
NT$	The new Taiwan dollar was established on June 15, 1949, with an exchange rate of NT$5 = U.S. $1. A multiple rate system was used for the new Taiwan dollar from 1950-59. A single certificate rate (NT$40 = U.S. $1) was adopted in June, 1959, and a unitary rate adopted in September, 1963, with the abolition of the foreign exchange certificate. (For further details, see Inter-National Financial Statistics (Washington, D.C.), various issues.)
1949 constant NT$	The new Taiwan dollar as a unit of measure in the years after 1949 was converted in terms of the purchasing power of the 1949 NT$ for purposes of making comparisons over time in this study.
T$	The Taiwan dollar before June 15, 1949.
1935-37 constant T$	The Taiwan dollar as a unit of measure was converted in terms of the average purchasing power of the 1935-37 T$.
. . .	Indicates lack of statistical data.

The Role of Land Reform in Economic Development

CHAPTER 1 INTRODUCTION

AN APPROACH TO THE PROBLEM

Few social arrangements have affected so many people for so long in man's history as the law and custom governing the ownership and use of land. The importance of the problem continues, if only because most people in the world still are directly dependent upon agriculture. This is especially so in the underdeveloped countries in the Far East. For example, in Thailand, India, and the Philippines, the agricultural population is 82,74, and 61 per cent, respectively, of the economically active total in the 1960's.[1] For these areas, agriculture still dominates the whole economy.

Continuous agricultural development can only be expected to occur under certain conditions of agrarian structure. A tenure system which is no longer in accord with the stage of political and economic development and which lacks a framework for adjustment will inevitably hinder development and foment political and social instability. Throughout history, discontented peasants have time and again helped topple governments which refused to initiate agrarian reforms.

The recent division of a large part of the world into two camps and the rising aspirations of the peoples in the underdeveloped areas for a better standard of living have kept the issue of land reform in the forefront. In siphoning off political and social tensions which discourage long-term investment, land reform is also said to have the beneficial effect of creating institutional preconditions for economic development. It is not uncommon in the discussion of economic development of agrarian countries to include a reference to the desirability of land reform.[2] However, the ways and the extent to which land reform will affect development are seldom spelled out in scientifically testable relations among empirically identifiable factors.

1

One reason for the lack of such study is perhaps that land reform[3] takes the nature of an innovation in the social order. It changes the organizational and structural framework within which economic activities occur, whereas existing economic theories usually assume that the institutional framework is to be held stable in order that analyses can be reduced to manageable proportions.[4]

In this study, we recognize that land reform, like any policy change, affects some persons favorably and others adversely and, as such, is part of the foundation of welfare economics. So far all theoretical attempts to construct a rigorous and universally applicable criterion for distinguishing what policy change is an economic improvement have floundered on the problem of interpersonal comparison of satisfaction, because there is no a priori way to evaluate the effect of the policy change. The only reasonable solution to the social-welfare problem is the formulation of a set of explicit value judgments which enable the analyst to examine the situation.[5] This recognition allows us to specify the distinctive aspects of the role of land reform in economic development that should be measured.

The aspects most easily perceived and measured are the primary effects of land reform (i.e., rent reduction, sale of public land, and land-to-the-tiller program). They consist of the means of compensation to the ex-landowners, the extent of land redistribution with consequent fragmentation of land-holdings, and the size of income transfer following rent reduction. The focus is clearly on the income distribution, assuming that the size of the national income remains constant. The transfer of rental income from large landowners to the cultivators will necessarily affect the prevailing balance between saving and consumption. This brings us to the secondary effects of land reform or, more aptly, to the question of its impact on enlarging the size of the national income. Detailed knowledge of saving and consumption in the two strata of the agricultural population is seldom available, but without this knowledge, it is impossible to know precisely the relative disposition of their share in the national income. Fortunately, the effect of income redistribution on economic development need not be appraised exclusively in terms of consumption and saving. In the less developed countries, the savings of the landowners are not necessarily used for productive investment, and in this case, a redistribution of income may not reduce the total investment. Even when savings are usually productively invested, changes arising from measures limited strictly to a redistribution of agricultural income according to actual contribution to production should give incentive to an increase in productivity which is measureable. Thus, we shall devote much of our discussion to assessing the increase of productivity of the agricultural sector and of the major crops and the impact of the change of farm size on productivity.

Another interesting secondary effect of land reform is the disposition of funds acquired by the landowners after they have sold their land. Industrialization in Taiwan will be fostered if they invest such funds in industrial and urban development. Here the difficulty in getting an answer lies as much in lack of data as in our analytic methods. In considering the secondary effects of land reform, or any policy decision, on economic development, we must recognize the difficulty of disentangling the effects of the reform from those of other changes. Since the land reform measures are a part of the general economic and social policies of the government, the achievements cannot be fully attributable to land reform but are contingent upon what decisions were taken on other economic and social policies. Thus, even if we deal with the increased income of the agricultural sector or productivity of major crops in the years immediately following the land reform and limit our observations to only the crops grown on the land subject to rent reduction or purchased by the owner cultivators, the magnitude and measurement of the output and the productivity so measured still depend upon the rest of the economy. If such a note of caution needs to be sounded when discussing the secondary effects, far greater care should be exercised when considering the tertiary effects of land reform.

It is true that rent reduction or limitation acts as an incentive to the peasants to work harder, and the land-to-the-tiller program promises a reward to the peasants for their efforts. In the nature of things, the peasants will question (and who will not?) whether these programs imply or signal that all hard work and sacrifice on their part will be rewarded. For example, if they save more, will such savings be protected against inflation and be rewarded at a reasonable rate of return? More importantly, should they reduce consumption on "luxuries" and put their children through school and would they get as much of a chance for upward mobility in the society as the other children of similar ability? In essence, can they improve their livelihood and/or their children's by hard work and self-denial? If the peasants are sufficiently convinced that their limited experience can be generalized into the norm of expectation, we shall have a generalized chain effect in the incentive system. We speak of a chain effect because we are concerned not with a single, once-and-for-all change which exhausts itself, but with something which goes on so that each phase contains the germ for further incentive. It is generalized because it requires, or results in, changes in beliefs, attitudes, relationships, institutions, and organizations not usually thought of as economic, or at least not entirely so.

A generalized incentive effect, if it should prevail, is an extremely important step in fostering economic development but it is not subject to quantitative measurement. Instead, we shall examine the flow of funds from the agricultural to the nonagricultural sectors and the size of out-migration from the farm as approximate indications or proxy variables of such changes of attitudes in the farming community. However, it should be noted that even if there is no outflow of funds from the agricultural to the nonagricultural sectors, the purchasing power transferred by the ex-landlords to the cultivators should not be considered as consumed or as having made no contribution to enlarging the flow of output in the years to come. If additional income was made possible for the cultivators to eat more, get better housing, and enjoy some medical care, it should be considered as an urgently needed investment in human capital. Even with the best equipment, land, and technology, it is hard to achieve high productivity if the human agent is in a miserable state.

As a final assessment, the returns from land reform are judged against opportunity cost. We believe that evaluations of social and economic changes such as land reform have meaning only with respect to the particular end or set of ends being considered. This is not to say that all studies on land reform should have the same end upon which success or failure is judged, but a decision regarding which goal should properly be allowed to refer to the welfare of the community as a whole and which should not must be sought in the value judgment by the author. Finally, any such grouping of the impact of land reform into primary, secondary, and tertiary effects as well as measurable and nonmeasurable factors necessarily contains an element of arbitrariness and ambiguity. But as long as we keep the semantic caution in mind, our framework for structuring the materials is perhaps just as satisfactory as any others. The analysis will be based on statistical data because economic development is essentially a quantitative concept. Some idea of the magnitude of the economic change is indispensable for clear understanding and analysis of the role of land reform in economic development.

The study unfolds in the following sequence: After a brief introduction of Taiwan in the next section of this chapter, the development of Taiwan economy from 1895 to 1945 is reviewed in Chapter 2. This serves as a background for later evaluation of the extent of contribution of the land reform program. Chapter 3 presents the major achievements of the land reform during the period 1949-53. In Chapter 4, the impact of land reform on the income of cultivators is examined as well as the disposition of funds by former landowners. Chapter 5 discusses the impact of land reform on output and income of the agricultural sector and land productivity based on the data of the agricultural sector and of the major crops. The effect of the size of holdings on land productivity is reviewed in the light of recent Taiwan experience. The question of financing development through agricultural surplus is discussed in Chapter 6, and the question of disguised unemployment and labor mobility in Chapter 7. Chapter 8 attempts to take into account the money and opportunity costs of land reform in Taiwan as a basis for assessing land reform as an instrument of government policy for economic development. Chapter 9 presents the summary and conclusion of the study.

TAIWAN

Taiwan, better known as "Formosa" in the Western world, is a tobacco-leaf-shaped island in the western Pacific Ocean, spanning the Tropic of Cancer. It was retrocessed to China in 1945 from Japanese control and has since been a province. It is 240 miles long from north to south and about 85 miles at its greatest width. Its area, including adjacent islands, is 35,961 square kilometers, or 13,885 square miles. The island is predominantly mountainous. More than two thirds of the land is composed of steep, rugged foothill ranges and massive mountain chains with peaks exceeding an elevation of 12,975 feet. These mountain ranges divide the rocky and rugged east coast from the fertile plains of the west. Cultivable land totals about 880,000 hectares (about 25 per cent of the total area), almost all of which has been fully cultivated.[6]

Taiwan has a generally warm climate, with heavy rainfalls, frequent strong winds, long and hot summers, and short and mild winters. The climate is subtropical in the north and tropical in the south. Crops can be grown all year round except in high mountain areas where freezing temperatures sometimes occur. Frost is rare on the plains. The annual rainfall, 1,500 to 2,000 millimeters on the plains, is sufficient for most crops. The distribution of rainfall, however, is uneven. Heavy rainfall occurs especially during the typhoon season, which lasts from May to October and often brings damage to the land and crops.

The major crops are rice and sugar cane. Secondary crops are sweet potatoes, tea, fruit, and peanuts. Of total exports the percentage of agricultural produce has always been high, varying from almost 90 per cent in the early 1950's to a little over 60 per cent in the 1960's. This drastic reduction of the percentage is due partly to a drop in the price of sugar, which dominates the agricultural exports.

The statistics of household registration showed the 1961 population to be more than 11.1 million (excluding armed forces). The annual rate of natural population increase (3.6 per cent) and the density of population (310 per square kilometer, or 802 per square mile) are among the highest in the world today.[7] A little less than 50 per cent of the population (5.4 million) is classified as agricultural and produces about one third of the net national product. In this and many other respects, Taiwan fits the usual description of an underdeveloped economy.

Since Taiwan is an island, the movements of men and goods in and out have been systematically recorded since 1895. Other economic statistics on agriculture, industrial production, and public finance are reasonably reliable.[8] In a real sense, here is a laboratory case for the study of the problem of economic development.

Taiwan has undergone two distinct stages of development, chiefly in connection with agriculture. In the first phase, the Japanese Government introduced and extended modern agricultural technology in Taiwan (which was under Japanese control from 1895-1945). Large-scale development of water resources as well as technological improvement in rice and sugar-cane production were promoted. The second phase mainly concerns the impetus to agriculture provided by the land reform, instituted after 1945. First, there was a program of rent reduction in 1949, followed by sale of public land in 1951 and a land-to-the-tiller program in 1953. These two main phases form the subject matter of separate chapters that follow.

CHAPTER **2** AGRICULTURAL
DEVELOPMENT,
1895-1945

From 1895 to the end of World War II, the strategy of development in Taiwan and its achievements were impressive: One only needs to look at the agricultural output which underwent continuous expansion. Excluding the war years of 1941-45, per capita income of the agricultural sector almost doubled, despite the fact that the agricultural population increased by approximately 43 per cent.[1] Given the overwhelming importance of agriculture, per capita income of this sector substantially reflected the thrust of the economy. This is impressive because Taiwan had few natural advantages in the way of abundant mineral or energy resources.

The strategy of development placed primary emphasis on agriculture, especially on the production of rice and sugar cane. This emphasis is mainly attributable to the fact that from 1895 to 1945, Taiwan was under the control of Japan, where these commodities were in great demand. With an assured export market, enough foreign exchange was generated so that the development was financed with little or no foreign capital.

The immediate concern of the present chapter is to view the land reform program (which will be described in Chapter 3) from an historical perspective. Thus, we focus our attention on the agricultural achievement. The story unfolds in three parts: (1) the initial efforts directed toward improving the economic environment, making it more favorable to development and investment in social overhead; (2) specific measures designed to increase the output of both rice and sugar in order to minimize their competition for land resources; and (3) the strategy of accumulating domestic savings and importing little or no foreign (Japanese) capital for development. The last point is demonstrated by constructing and assessing the annual balance of payments of Taiwan for half a century.

GROUNDWORK FOR DEVELOPMENT

Several measures of economic significance initiated during this period are worthy of mention. Thanks to the efficient and forceful administration of these programs, they were successfully implemented and have since been milestones of development.[2] When Japan took over Taiwan, steps were immediately taken to commercialize the produce of Taiwan. In a mass exchange economy, commodities must be specified in terms of uniform physical and monetary units. In October, 1895, the standard Japanese instruments of weights and measurement were introduced and were then decreed as the official system for Taiwan in 1900. The old standards of measurement were prohibited by the end of 1903. Beginning in 1904, all items related to the manufacture, maintenance, repair, and sale of weights and measures were monopolized by the government.

Japan adopted the gold standard in 1897. Efforts were made for an immediate extension of the system to Taiwan. Under a set price between silver and gold, the silver dollar was first declared as legal tender. When the Bank of Taiwan was established in 1899, bank notes redeemable in silver and gold caused complications in accounting procedures and brought about uncertainty and injustice in business transactions between merchants in Japan and Taiwan. Accordingly, in June, 1904, the Bank of Taiwan was authorized to issue gold notes. Except for paying taxes, silver dollars and notes were prohibited. By 1905, they were declared unacceptable for paying taxes. The currency system of Taiwan was completely integrated with that of Japan by 1911,[3] and this removed the exchange rate problem for Japan in trading between the two. In addition, the monetary arrangement required the banks in Taiwan to keep their currency reserves in Japan and made Japan the recipient of capital from Taiwan for a quantitatively significant sum. This point shall be examined in relation to the balance of payments of Taiwan. The monetary reform did little, however, to stabilize the agricultural prices.[4]

A more tangible contributing factor to the development during the period was a continuous inflow of Japanese technical and professional personnel to Taiwan. The government hired most of its key staff in the government schools and the university from Japan. The turnover rate, as reflected in the statistics of Japanese nationals coming to Taiwan and leaving, however, was high. Thus, gross figures would be quite misleading. A net flow of Japanese nationals classified according to such professions as farming, commerce, industry, civil service and independent professionals, etc., is presented in Table 1 for the period 1897–1942.

Table 1
Japanese Immigrants to Taiwan (Net), 1897–1942
(Unit: Number of persons)

Year	Agriculture & Fishery	Mining & Industry	Commerce & Communication	Civil Service & Professional	Others	Sum
1897–99 (3 years)	2,481	6,140	20,238	7,614	15,082	51,555
1900–09	6,424	1,929	7,941	5,470	16,902	38,666
1910–19	17,917	1,874	10,000	12,342	59,626	101,759
1920–29	4,076	2,750	15,166	16,833	42,297	81,122
1930–39	11,955	6,101	23,713	23,553	31,565	96,887
1940–42 (3 years)	2,964	5,240	10,400	12,623	26,984	58,211

Source: *Statistical Abstract of Taiwan Province During the Fifty-one Year Period* (in Chinese) (Taipei, 1946), Table 95.

Counting the talents of immigrants, commerce and communication people stood out as the largest single group from the beginning. In the decade of 1910–19, agriculture and fishery headed the list with nearly 18,000 persons. The lead switched during the 1920's to civil servants and professionals with nearly 17,000 persons. The sequence roughly corresponded to the pattern of initial investment in social overhead of road and harbor construction and establishment of basic business organizations. Then came the time of intensive agricultural development and general expansion of demand for government and other professional services. However, the importance of the inflow cannot be measured solely in terms of the absolute number of persons. To give a feeling for their role in the development process, we must assess their proportion in relation to the total manpower in each profession. The censuses on population taken for the years 1904, 1915, 1920, and 1930 gave a detailed breakdown of the number of Japanese in each profession. Table 2 shows the percentages. One will note that civil service personnel ranked the highest in the major classifications for all four census years, followed by educational personnel in the last two censuses when there was a separate category for them. The listing of percentages for the major professional groups has blurred many interesting details of the picture. As an illustration, the per cent of civil engineers in industry was always high and above the industrial average. The percentage distribution for this subgroup was: 1904, 29 per cent; 1915, 38 per cent; 1920, 24 per cent; and 1930, 14 per cent. This information confirms our earlier conjecture on the major social overhead investment during the early years of Japanese control, consisting of the completion of the North-South Cross Island Railway, linking Keelung and Kaohsiung in 1908; construction of the first major port at Keelung; and a network of road systems.

Table 2
Composition of Japanese in
Various Professions for Selected Years
(Percentage of Total Reported in Each Profession)
(Unit: Percentage)

Professions	1904	1915	1920	1930
Agriculture and Forestry	0.03	0.39	0.35	0.37
Fishery	0.52	2.13	4.83	5.65
Mining	1.61	10.86	6.71	2.11
Industries	7.42	13.11	12.75	9.61
Commerce	7.09	12.10	13.43	10.16
Communication	13.39	16.49	16.60	14.35
Civil Service	52.19	62.40	57.16	66.11
Education	n.a.*	n.a.*	39.48	50.63

*n.a. indicates no figures available

Source: *Statistical Abstract of Taiwan Province During the Fifty-one Year Period* (in Chinese) (Taipei, 1946), Table 59.

The work directly related to agriculture was the establishment of a cadastral system, under which the categories, grades, and areas of land were duly investigated and surveyed, and

A summary of expenditures for irrigation from 1901–60 (by decades) is shown in Table 3. The data give a breakdown between investment and operational outlays (repairs, maintenance, and administrative expenses). But within the investment category, no satisfactory further allocation between new projects and replacement is feasible. In order to eliminate money value changes, they are deflated by the price index (1935–37 price index equals 100). Only direct government expenditures devoted to irrigation and expenditures by the irrigation associations are included. In the absence of private expenditures by farmers on irrigation facilities, the figures, therefore, generally represent an understatement of the actual costs. A rough indication of the contribution of individual farmers is the ratio of self-installed to public-installed irrigation facilities. In the *Report on the 1956 Sample Census of Agriculture*, 12 per cent of irrigated acreage was self-installed. Another element of understatement is the free labor commandeered by the government for some parts of the construction work.

Table 3

Outlays for Irrigation by Government and Irrigation Associations, by Decades

(Unit: 1935–37 Taiwan dollars)

Decades	Total Investment (in $1,000)	Per Cent by Government	Per Cent by Irrigation Association	Operational Outlay (in $1,000)	Total Investment and Operational Outlays (in $1,000)
1901–10	6,230	92	8	9,417	15,647
1911–20	9,457	91	9	19,049	28,506
1921–30	81,765	35	65	131,438	213,203
1931–40	24,710	31	69	93,569	118,279
1941–50	19,861	2	98	50,091	69,952
1951–60	21,168	45	55	47,902	69,070

Source: E. L. Rada and T. H. Lee, *Irrigation Investment in Taiwan* (Taipei: Sino-American Joint Commission on Rural Reconstruction, 1963), p. 37.

The reported investments (government and irrigation associations) rose from T$6.2 million in the decade of 1901–10 to a peak of T$81 million in 1921–30, both in 1935–37 Taiwan dollars. The pattern for operational outlays is similar. However, the share contributed by the government declined decade by decade as the irrigation associations increasingly took over the responsibility. The policy of gradual withdrawal of the government's support in such investment has definite merit. In the early years of agricultural development, investment in irrigation was risky and the expected yield uncertain. Hence, the leadership role of the government was much needed. As experience multiplied, the risk became minimal, and private investors were encouraged to take over. The resources of the government so freed were thus made available to be used in new fields where government pioneering could accelerate the rate of growth.

RESEARCH AND THE DISSEMINATION OF AGRICULTURAL TECHNOLOGY

The work of seed improvement of Chailai rice, a local variety, was started by the Taipei Agricultural Experimental Station in 1899 and joined later by various research agencies supported by the government. The most notable achievement of the research, however, was the introduction and adaptation of Ponlai rice to the local conditions in Taiwan. Successful planting was initially limited to the Taipei area where the climatic condition is similar to that of the northern plateau of Japan. Beginning in 1926, when a new breeding method was discovered, the planting of Ponlai rice gradually moved from the high plateaus to the sea-level area, thus making possible the spread of Ponlai rice fields from northern Taiwan to the south and from one crop to more than one.[8]

In addition to seed selection, the application of fertilizers contributes greatly to the increase of the yield of rice. The spread of the knowledge of fertilizer utilization is due in large measure to the work of the sugar mills, which undertook extensive campaigns to educate the farmers. At a very early stage, the sugar mills had to pass out fertilizers to the farmers free of charge because most of the farmers had little knowledge of the value of fertilizers and refused to use them when they had to pay for them. After 1903, a subsidy was granted to farmers for fertilizer purchase. All the functions of importation and distribution were undertaken by the sugar mills. The subsidy was discontinued in 1916, but the sugar fields under the direct control of the sugar mills continued experimenting with the techniques of fertilizer application. Thus, the extensive use of fertilizers in Taiwan farming started largely under the

promotion of the sugar mills and then spread to other crops.
In the course of forty-five years, the application of fertilizers
to rice increased by more than two and a half times.[9]

The intensive use of fertilizers and popularization of the
Ponlai rice seemed to move hand in hand. In an experimental
study of the effects of fertilizer application to two types of
rice, the Ponlai variety responded to the fertilizer treatment
much more sharply than Chailai.[10]   Clearly, the discovery of
the Ponlai variety was a major breakthrough in rice production,
an innovation of greatest importance for the Taiwan economy.
There remained the job of quick dissemination. Fortunately,
keeping farmers informed of improved methods of production
was undertaken early through an extensive network of agricultural associations.[11] Some examples are: the introduction
of community rice nurseries in the Kaohsiung and Taichung
area in 1907, encouragement to grow green manure crops in
1908, institution of the two-crop system in the Taitung-Hwalien
area in 1919, and the introduction of dense planting to the
island in 1922. By 1925, these practices spread to all areas
and the farmers were eager and ready to adopt the new rice
variety.

The efforts described above were reflected in rising rice
yields per hectare which increased from an average of 1,280
kilograms in the 1900's to 1,930 kilograms in the 1930's.
Japan, being the chief beneficiary, imported 76,000 metric tons
of rice a year in the former period, or 14 per cent of total
production, and 576,000 metric tons a year, or 46 per cent of
the total production in the 1930's. This means Japan took
practically the entire rice export from Taiwan. In terms of
percentage, it was 84 per cent in the 1900's with an increase
to 99 per cent in the ensuing three decades, as shown in Table
4.

PROMOTION OF SUGAR PRODUCTION

In 1902, the Sugar Industry Encouragement Act was promulgated, under which various forms of subsidy were to be
given to the sugar-cane producers for expenditures incurred
in developing sugar-cane plantations, irrigation and drainage
of sugar-cane fields, breeding of better species, and introduction of fertilizers, etc. Other measures included the free grant

Table 4

Average Rice Production and Exports to Japan, by Decades

Year	(1) Output (1,000 MT)	(2) Exports to Japan (1,000 MT)	(3) (2)/(1) Percentage	(4) Exports to Japan as Percentage of Total Exports
1900–09	543	76	14.0	84.0
1910–19	690	119	17.2	98.6
1920–29	787	250	31.7	99.8
1930–39	1,258	576	45.8	99.4

Source: *Economic History of Taiwan During the Period of Japanese Control* (in Chinese), Vol. I (Bureau of Economic Research, Bank of Taiwan, 1958), pp. 37, 140–41, 147–48.

of government land for sugar-cane plantations and the availability of low interest rate loans from the Bank of Taiwan for financing exports. In addition to the economic incentive, some coercion was used.[12]

The result of the efforts was substantial. In the forty-year period, beginning 1902, the planting area increased from 16,029 hectares to 107,676 hectares, or an increase of 67.2 per cent. The highest year was 1939–40 with a total of 169,048 hectares; compared with the figure in 1902–03, it was a 1,055 per cent increase. The output increased from 409 million kilograms to 4,159 million kilograms, or 1,015 per cent increase. The per hectare yield rose from 25,572 kilograms to 38,628 kilograms, or 151 per cent increase. The per hectare yield was highest in 1938–39, totaling 79,039 kilograms. Compared with the figure in 1902–03, it was a 305 per cent increase. But the efficient operation of plants is largely conditioned by the continuity of the supply of raw materials. To ensure this, the Regulations Governing the Establishment of Sugar-Manufacturing Plants were promulgated in 1905. Henceforth, no plant could be set up without the approval of the government. The island was zoned for the purpose of allocating sugar cane among the sugar producers, and the supply within each district was prohibited from being shipped outside the district. On the other hand, if the sugar mills failed to buy all the supplies within their allocated districts, they would be subject to penalty assessments. The decision of how much sugar cane to plant was supposedly left with the farmers, who would choose among the competing crops for the use of land after having learned the purchase price of sugar cane as announced by the sugar mills. The purchase price of sugar cane, incidentally, did not depend upon the price of sugar but upon the price of rice, the main crop that competed with the sugar cane from the supply side for the use of land. The economic implications of this behavior of sugar firms will be discussed later in this section.

Although the growth of the sugar industry in Taiwan was not due to any single cause, the promotion on the part of the government was certainly a great help. From 1903 to 1925, a total of T$127 million was paid out by the government as subsidy, in addition to the free distribution of 2,460 million sugar-cane plants. Indirect costs of administration and implementation amounted to T$120 million, but the dividend was handsome. From Japan's point of view, a domestic source of sugar supply was assured, with considerable saving of its foreign exchange.

From 1894 to 1944, sugar production in Taiwan increased from 55,253 metric tons to 327,199 metric tons or by 592 per cent. But the year of highest production was 1938 when the output was 1,418,730 metric tons. The decline since then was due to the war economy. The sugar export from Taiwan increased from 25,927 metric tons in 1901 to 243,650 metric tons in 1944, or 935 per cent. 1939 witnessed the largest export, i.e., 1,153,920 metric tons. In 1901 exports to Japan were 48 per cent of the total output and in 1944 they were 73 per cent. The average for the entire period was 85 per cent and the exports to Japan were on the average 94 per cent of total exports.

Credit for the rapid expansion of sugar output should also be given to the continuous improvement of the sugar-cane varieties. Dating back to about 1660, when sugar cane was first planted in Taiwan, one sugar-cane variety after another was adopted. Some came from abroad, such as the Rose Bamboo from Hawaii; others were discovered locally. In spite of the marked difference in yield between the newly discovered and prevailing varieties, time was needed to spread the knowledge and distribute the new variety to the farmers. In the meantime the average yield per hectare for Taiwan as a whole rose gradually but consistently.[13]

Up to the time of heavy-stalk sugar cane (POJ-2725 and kindred varieties), sugar-cane fields needed much less water

Table 5
Average Sugar Production and Exports to Japan,
by Decades

	(1)	(2)	(3)	(4)
Year	Output	Exports to Japan (MT)	(2)/(1) Percentage	Exports to Japan as Percentage of Total Exports
1894-1900	43,361	n.a.	...*	...
1901-10	98,274	65,409	71	93
1911-20	249,735	216,211	98	92
1921-30	552,807	478,587	87	97
1931-40	950,079	845,798	92	95
1941-45	840,672	564,827	67	84

* Indicates lack of statistical data.

Source: *Economic History of Taiwan During the Period of Japanese Control* (in Chinese), Vol. I (Bureau of Economic Research, Bank of Taiwan, 1958), pp. 79-80.

than rice fields for efficient production. Therefore, the well-irrigated fields of the northern and central parts of Taiwan were engaged in rice production, and the south, lacking water, specialized in sugar-cane production.

Since the introduction of heavy-stalk sugar cane to protect against wind storms, the story has been changed. This variety of sugar cane, like rice, also needs a lot of water. The paddy fields normally devoted to growing rice were in demand by both crops. Moreover, after the completion of the Chianan Canal, dry fields became paddy fields. This enlarged the land area substitutable for use in growing either crop and, thus, intensified the competition.

To the farmers who were able to cultivate either rice or sugar cane, the problem was to produce the crop that would yield the maximum gains. In the short run, the crop productivity and, accordingly, farm expenses were fixed and the supply of either crop was determined by the relative prices, current and expected, between rice and sugar cane, so that either crop should be equally profitable if the equilibrating process were allowed to work itself out. Direct evidence on production cost, receipts, and net profit and losses per hectare is available for quite a number of years, but it covers different periods for sugar cane and rice. Only in the 1926–27 period do we have figures for both sugar cane and rice. The net receipts are roughly comparable.[14]

The sugar producers on the island grew part of their sugar cane requirement in plantations owned by themselves. The remaining part was purchased from the farmers on contract. By law, no sugar cane could be shipped outside a district in which there was only one producer, as was the case in many districts. They were true monopolistic buyers (monoposonists). If not for the substitutability of rice and sugar growing, the price of sugar cane could be arbitrarily set to cover the cost of sugar-cane growers, with no reference to the price of sugar. But since rice could be cultivated instead of sugar cane on the same parcel of land, the buying price of sugar cane was set in relation to the price of rice, and this insured a continuous supply of raw material.[15] This was a good example of setting the price in accordance with the opportunity cost of the producers.[16]

From the point of view of the sugar manufacturers, the relationship between the sugar-cane price and the rice price added an element of uncertainty to their profit margin, especially when the cost of raw material occupied such a high fraction of the total cost.[17] In times of a rising sugar price and a falling rice price, the profit margin of sugar producer would be widened, and vice versa, in times of a falling sugar price and a rising rice price. Therefore, the relative price between rice and sugar is indicative of the relative rise or fall of the profit margins. The fall of the relative price of sugar from 1914 to 1943[18] resulted in a squeeze on the profit margin of the sugar manufacturers and perhaps accounted in part for the rapid rise of more efficient modern plants. But the squeeze was to some measure relieved by the increase in the yield of sugar cane relative to rice in the mills' own plantations.[19]

Close substitutability of land use for growing sugar cane or rice has implications beyond the profit margin of sugar mills. It made the supply of rice and sugar cane more responsive to price changes. Taiwan was indeed in the enviable position of having such flexibility in resource utilization between two major cash crops. In the long run, the terms of trade of a country are a matter of good fortune and the capacity to enter new industries and to quit the old. No one can do much about luck, but if a country has the capacity to shift its resources in response to changes in demand, its terms of trade will tend to be favorable despite average luck.[20]

FINANCING COST OF PROMOTION AND PUBLIC INVESTMENT

The main source of financing government promotion and public investment came from the annual budget for the whole island. In addition, the expenses for promoting enterprises were also incurred at the county and city government levels, but such figures are available only for the years since 1920. Measured in terms of the 1935-37 Taiwan dollar, there were marked yearly fluctuations with an upward trend (Table 6). The main items were for the construction and improvement of railroads, investment in establishing motor transportation, road construction, and water works.[21] The promotion expenses were spent on rice growing, silk cocoon and pineapple production, inspection of agricultural exports, and marine output. Subsidies went into marine navigation, private railroads,

Table 6
Public Investment and Government Subsidies, 1896-1944

Year	Total Public Investment and Subsidies (Excluding Expenditures Designed for Expansion into South China and the South Pacific Area) (Constant 1935-37 T$1,000)	Percentage of* Total Government Expenditure
1896-1905	104,458	45.02
1906-15	176,070	36.79
1916-25	146,228	35.86
1926-35	245,626	34.46
1936-44 (9 years)	309,377	34.63

*Government expenditure excluding outlays to cover expenses of such government enterprises as Bureaus of Communications and Monopoly.

Source: *Statistical Abstract of Taiwan Province During the Fifty-one Year Period* (in Chinese) (Taipei, 1946), Tables 336, 348, and 366.

civil aviation, oil-field exploration, and harbor improvement. Direct subsidy to the industries did not come into being until 1937. The percentage of such expenditures in terms of the total budget seemed to decline over the decades. It started with 45 per cent of the total provincial budget in the first decade 1896-1905 and declined to, and stabilized at, the level 35 per cent during and after the 1920's.

The proceeds from the sale of the government bonds were considered a receipt under the heading of nonrecurrent items. It was known that money so raised was used to finance major enterprises and construction works. But, except in the first decade, the money covered only a small fraction of such totals. Therefore, it is reasonable to assume that the amount of money for public investment not covered by such borrowing was financed from taxation and monopoly profits, as shown by the percentage distribution of government receipts in Table 7.

Table 7
Percentage Distribution of Government
Receipts, 1897-1941*

Year	Taxes	Government Property and Monopolies	Public Debt	Surplus from Previous Year	Others
1897-05 (9 years)	38.21	−5.04	28.39	8.66	29.37
1906-15	42.10	19.80	5.27	29.19	3.65
1916-25	32.55	20.58	8.09	33.70	5.29
1926-35	28.12	31.67	3.03	34.14	3.18
1936-41	28.07	28.74	1.91	31.25	10.52

*The percentage may not add to 100 because of rounding.

Source: *Economic History of Taiwan During the Period of Japanese Control* (in Chinese), Vol. I (Bureau of Economic Research, Bank of Taiwan, 1958), pp. 322-23.

Details of the tax structure since 1928 are available. In 1928, only 12 per cent of the total tax revenue was collected from income tax, and the balance came chiefly from land rent

(27 per cent), sugar consumption tax (14 per cent), wine and spirit tax (20 per cent), tea (2 per cent), and custom duty (22 per cent).[22] As late as 1941, the revenue from income tax was no higher than one third of the total tax receipts. The tax structure is a contrast to the doctrine of taxation based on the ability to pay. Moreover, upon examination of the items, included under government enterprises and monopolies, we find that the main source of revenue was from government monopolies. The budget had a surplus every year. On the other hand, it was not so with the government-owned enterprises, consisting mainly of railways and postal and telegraph services. Between 1887 and 1941, the railways and other enterprises related to communications had deficits for seventeen years; postal and telegraph services, for twenty years. Even in years when receipts from the monopoly profit and the government enterprises were both positive, the receipt from the former (T$ 44 million in 1941) was as much as ten times greater than the latter. Except for camphor, which was largely exported, the other items under government monopoly were salt, wine and spirits, and tobacco. Again, it must be stressed that the burden of such receipts had little relation with the ability to pay.

In order to assess the role of public investment, we need a picture of the total investment made by both the government and the private investors. There is no direct information on the annual investment in the private sector. We only have access to annual data on the capital stock and surplus of various business firms. However, by noting the differences of the yearly figures, we have a rough approximation to the annual investment. To even out any undue fluctuation of annual figures and to ascertain a long-term picture of private investment, we shall add them on a decade basis by first converting all the figures to the constant Taiwan dollars of 1935-37. When we express private investment as a fraction of the total investment (government and private),[23] we find that private investment was only 5 per cent in the early years, rose to 45 per cent in the second decade, and then rose to 65 per cent in the early 1920's. In the late 1920's and early 1930's, private investment suffered a sudden drop when the percentage went down to 27 per cent. Under the stimulus of war preparation, private investment went back to its high level of about 65 per cent in the late 1930's, up to the year immediately prior to the end of World War II. But for 1900-1950, private investment was only a little more than half of the total investment, or 52 per cent.

To what extent did foreign capital contribute to the economic development during the period of Japanese control? In order to get a systematic picture, we piece together, in as feasible a manner as possible, all relevant information for constructing the balance of payments of Taiwan from 1896 to 1944. Since there are many gaps and omissions in Appendix Table 11,[24] our discussion will be confined to the order of magnitude of the figures. The commodity account has been favorable since 1909. The surplus has been largely offset by the service account. The overseas ships were owned by foreigners (mostly, if not all, by Japanese firms).[25] The shipping charges included only the outgoing passenger portion and no allowance was made for goods because the commodity account was valued F.O.B. for exports and C.I.F. for imports. The other key item that absorbed the favorable balance on the commodity account was the import of currency and gold and silver bars, but such figures are not available for the years after 1937. Government transfers in and out of Taiwan took two opposite patterns in two periods. In the early years, 1896-1904, there was a financial subsidy of $30,485,000 in Taiwan currency from Japan. The amount decreased each year and came to a complete stop in 1905. The importance of this yearly subsidy to the development of Taiwan can be assessed in terms of its contribution to the total government receipts in those years. It started with as high a percentage as 72 per cent, declining to 3 per cent in 1904, the last year of the subsidy.[26]

Then came the period of Sino-Japanese hostilities in 1931-40 and World War II, when the government bonds of Japan were sold on a large scale in Taiwan.[27] There are no yearly details for the period 1931-37; the 1937 figure included all these years. The bond drive ended in 1944 according to the official statistics, and netted a total of $1,136,347,000 (i.e., the sum of years from 1931 to 1944). The other transfers were derived from the reported foreign exchange receipts, after appropriate adjustments for commodity and shipping services. To force the balance between receipts and payments, we have a category of accommodating capital movement which may well include errors and omissions which cannot be separated. However, the persistence of negative signs after 1918 and up to 1936 pointed to the outflow of short-term capital to Japan in the form of accumulated balances in the banks.

Since the Japanese yen was a reserve currency for its colonies, the banks in Taiwan had little choice but to maintain a sizable balance in Japan as a means of payment for Taiwan's foreign trade, which was largely with Japan. Because of the government bond subscription during 1937 and afterward, it may be safe to generalize that except for the first decade, there was little net inflow of foreign capital to Taiwan for its development.[28]

SUMMARY AND CONCLUSION

Taiwan started the process of economic development by committing itself to substantial social overhead costs in land survey, road and harbor construction, agricultural research and extension work. In promoting water conservation and irrigation projects and giving various forms of subsidy to the sugar and other related activities, the government pointed out profitable investment opportunities to private investors. The technical improvement of rice and sugar-cane varieties came at the right time for immediate dissemination and adoption.

The implications of these early measures on the land reform program are clear. A reliable cadastral system made an immediate implementation of the land reform program possible. More than money and manpower, it takes time to complete a cadastral survey, and time was essential for the implementation of the 1949 land reform in Taiwan. The early extension service to educate the farmers on better methods of seed selection, fertilizer application, and more effective use of water resources had a long-term effect. Such knowledge was later put to the fullest use by the farmers when they had the proper incentive, such as the rent limitation program of 1949. Moreover, because of past successful experiences, farmers became more receptive to adopt other new measures for productivity increase. The desire to increase land productivity on the part of the tenants, and their early exposure to some technical know-how, made the land reform program in Taiwan more than a mere redistribution of income between the landlords and tenants. It explains in a large measure the increases in agricultural output and land productivity. This conclusion will be more fully documented in Chapter 5.

Profit from government monopolies and from consumption taxes provided the bulk of investment funds and exports of sugar and rice with the necessary foreign exchange for development. The story of the economic development in Taiwan during this period can be briefly summarized as an example of a successful combination of circumstances, namely, shrewd utilization of indigenous resources, fiscal manipulation to achieve forced savings, a few fortunate developments in agricultural research, and years of rising market for its exports, with the average citizens bearing the brunt of the burden of financing.

CHAPTER 3 LAND REFORM SINCE RETROCESSION

Scarcity and uneven distribution of farmland has long been the most serious problem encountered by the farmers in most parts of China. Taiwan is no exception. The classic example frequently cited about conditions on the farm is contained in an 1872 edition of the history of Pa-ling, modern Yueh-yang, the northern Hunan port:

> If the land (of the locality) is divided into ten portions, mountains and streams take up seven. If the population is divided into ten portions, scholars and merchants occupy four. If the agricultural population is divided into ten portions, tenants constitute six. If the agricultural population is divided into ten portions, daily necessities eat up one-half (of the total).[1]

With some slight changes in percentages, the description may hold for Taiwan during the nineteenth century.

In Taiwan, the pressure of population on land was held in check when the doubling of the population was almost matched by a commensurate increase of the farmland from 1905 to 1945.[2] Tenancy conditions never received as much attention as they deserved during the period of Japanese control. In fact, available evidence seems to suggest that the tenancy problem became increasingly more serious. The first census of population showing farmlandownership was taken in 1910. The tenant farmers were 42.8 per cent and part-owners comprised 23.5 per cent, making a total of 66.3 per cent. The percentage distribution moved slightly higher for tenant farmers at the time of the retrocession of Taiwan to China in 1945. The number of tenant farmers was about 70 per cent (39 per cent tenant farmers and 31 per cent part-owners).[3] In terms of the

27

area of land distribution between owners and tenant farmers there was also a slight shift from 1923 on, when such figures first became available. Forty-two per cent of the farmland was cultivated by the owners and 58 per cent by tenants. In 1939 the percentage became 44 per cent and 56 per cent, respectively.[4]

To fully appreciate the urgency of land reform in the late 1940's, some knowledge of Taiwan agriculture is essential. Briefly stated, the Taiwan agriculture has been characterized by land-intensive farming and abundant labor input.

A LAND-SCARCE AND LABOR-ABUNDANT AGRICULTURE

The subtropical and tropical climates in Taiwan permit the production of three or four crops a year on the same piece of land. Different varieties of crops (such as rice, sweet potatoes, corn, soybeans, and peanuts) can be grown in different seasons or months of the year. Therefore, as a cultural practice, systems of multiple cropping have been developed together with intercropping. It is a special feature of Taiwan agriculture. Take rice, the most important single crop, as an example.[5] Rice-growing periods in Taiwan vary with regions and varieties. In irrigated areas two crops of rice a year are harvested. The first crop is seeded and transplanted from December through March and harvested from May through July. The second crop is seeded and transplanted from June through August and harvested from late September through early December. The time of transplanting and harvesting is earlier in the south than in the north. Between the two rice crops, the field is utilized for summer and winter crops through relay planting, i.e., interplanting a new crop before the growing crop is harvested, as shown in Table 8. Jute, for example, is seeded between the rows of rice in the middle of April, about six weeks before the harvesting of rice. Winter crops consist chiefly of wheat, barley, tobacco, corn, and miscellaneous vegetables.

Nonirrigated regions raise only a single rice crop during the rainy summer, transplanting in May and June and harvesting in September or October. Peanuts, sweet potatoes, vegetables, or green manure crops are planted in between. Under the system of multiple cropping, what is emphasized is not only yield of a single crop but the total yield of three or more crops

Table 8
Multiple Cropping System on Paddy Fields

Number of Crops	Period from Planting or Transplanting to Harvesting
1. The first rice crop	February to June
2. Summer crops	
Jute	Mid-April to early August (relay planting)
Melon	Late May to early August (relay planting)
Oriental pickling melon	Early June to early August (relay planting)
Chinese cabbage	June to July
Soybeans	Early June to late July
Sesbania (green manure)	June to early August
Watermelon (for seeds)	Late May to early August
3. The second rice crop	August to October
4. Winter crops	
Wheat	Late October to late February
Barley	Late October to late February
Tobacco	Mid-September to early February (relay planting)
Rape	Mid-October to early March
Corn	Mid-October to early February
Soybeans	Mid-October to mid-February
Flax	Late October to early March
Vegetables (miscellaneous)	Mid-October to mid-February

Source: T. H. Shen, *Agriculture Development in Taiwan Since World War II* (Ithaca, N.Y.: Comstock Publishing Associates, 1964), p. 162.

a year for a given piece of land. For example, Taichung 31 wheat yields slightly less than Taichung 32 but matures three to five days earlier.[6] Farmers prefer Taichung 31, because an earlier harvest gives them a few extra days to prepare the ground more thoroughly for rice transplantation.

One way of summarizing the extensiveness of the multiple-cropping practice in Taiwan is to construct an index of the ratio between total crop area and total cultivated land area. An index of 100 means no multiple-cropping land. The indexes so constructed for the selected years show a consistently higher figure each year: 133 in 1939, 166 in 1949, and 182 in 1959.[7] The over-all figure conceals many interesting details. The regional difference of the multiple-cropping indexes is significant. The indexes for central Taiwan, where most of the fields are irrigated, are higher (212 in 1950) than those for southern Taiwan (162). Sugar cane, a major crop in southern Taiwan, and pineapples, which are grown for eighteen months, tend to lower the over-all index in the south.

One of the factors that determine the extent of multiple cropping and the kind of crops to be planted in Taiwan is irrigation. In partially irrigated districts where there is not enough water to irrigate the fields, a three-year rotation system is adopted so as to use one third of land each for growing rice, sugar cane, and sweet potatoes (or other crops). Rice is irrigated from May or June to September or October, sugar cane gets its share of irrigation for the rest of the year, and sweet potatoes receive none.

In addition to the heavy labor demand for seeding, transplanting, and harvesting the crops, the year-round cropping system in Taiwan needs labor to replenish large quantities of plant materials into the soil. Most soils in Taiwan are of loamy texture and, with few local exceptions, do not offer problems of poor drainage or difficulty in tillage. But the amounts of organic matter and materials in Taiwan soils are relatively low not only because of multiple cropping but also because of the speeding up of the organic matter, the weathering of minerals, and the leaching of nutrients by the tropical climate. Sound soil management demands a good portion of farm labor in growing green manure, preparing compost, and mulching in the dry season for crops such as pineapple, sugar cane, and citrus fruit, and in undertaking soil conservation measures, such as the construction of bench terraces on sloping land. Another labor-consuming job is the frequent application of chemical fertilizer, and, last but not least, the control of insects and plant diseases calls for the periodic spreading of insecticides. With a cultural practice such as this, extra efforts and care by the farmers make the difference in the yield, but such marginal exertions will not be forthcoming unless the farmers work under a land tenure system that gives them appropriate recognition and fair reward.

Unfortunately, prior to land reform, there had developed a land tenure system under which the average farmland rental was kept at approximately 50 per cent of the total annual main crop yield. It ran as high as 70 per cent in the more fertile areas. In addition, there was an arrangement known as "iron-clad" rent, by which, irrespective of good or bad harvest or of natural disasters, the tenant was required to pay a certain amount of rent. There was also a rent on farm by-products, payable in some cases in the same ratio as the regular rent. Only a very few lease contracts were either written or for specified periods of time. Instances of subleasing by tenants to other tenants were also common. This led to a cumulative form of exploitation. Extortions in the form of security deposits, guarantee money, and payment of rent in advance were also prevalent. The picture of these tenants on the eve of land reform was bleak indeed.

FARMLAND RENT REDUCTION

Land reform in the rural areas of Taiwan proceeded by stages, of which rent reduction was the initial one. Arrangements for implementing the program started in January, 1949, and actual enforcement began in April. It limited farm rent to a maximum of 37.5 per cent of the total main crop yield. The figure 37.5 per cent was arrived at by taking one quarter of the total annual yield as the tenant's share and then dividing the remaining three quarters equally between landlord and tenant. Since the farm rent reduction was based on the total annual yield of the principal crop, the degree of accuracy with which the amount of the total annual yield was appraised would obviously have a direct bearing on enforcement and on the success or failure of the program itself. Past experience ruled out such devices as leaving the appraisal to the landlord and his tenant to agree on a figure or to take the actual harvest figure, because it was difficult, if at all possible, to arrive at a consensus. Even if some sort of compromise were reached, it was questionable that the appraisal would be strictly fair in view of the disparity in bargaining power between the two.

Fortunately, in Taiwan there is a working cadastral system, under which the categories, grades, and areas of land have been duly investigated, surveyed, and the land rights registered. It was done long before the institution of the land reform, so there was no question as to its objectivity. The results were accepted by the landlords and the tenants. This made it possible for the government to step in to establish a standard yield for every grade of paddy field (including single and double fields and three-year rotation fields) and dry land in every *hsien* (county) and city. There are certain dry lands which are devoted throughout the year to special crops, such as tea, fruits, citronella, etc. Owing to the small fraction of such lands and to the low rental rates originally charged, the new rental rates were left to be negotiated by and agreed upon between the landlords and tenants, following the general principle of the rent reduction program.

At the same time, all extra burdens, such as advance rent payments and security deposits, were abolished. In the case of crop failure caused by natural disaster, rent reduction or remission in proportion to the degree of damage to the crop might be permitted.

The revision of farm lease contracts in Taiwan was carried out as part of the procedure for negotiation according to the regulations for rent reduction. In this way, all farm lease contracts were written. It was further provided by law that the lease period should not be shorter than six years. For the duration of the contract, the landlord might not, except for legally specified reasons, such as arrears in excess of two years' rent, terminate the contract. If, at the end of the lease period, the lessee were willing to continue the lease, the contract would have to be renewed, unless the lessor would take back the land for his own cultivation.

Contracts for private farmland under lease that had been duly revised by June, 1949, totaled 377,364. The figure marked the formal completion of the first phase of the rent reduction program. The follow-up program included spot inspection and rechecking by the Taiwan Provincial Government for possible violations of the new lease terms. In view of the number of irregularities discovered and duly corrected (34,867 cases), [8] the practical significance of the rechecking program should not be overlooked.

The above record of achievement was reflected by a market test of the value of the farmland before and after the institution of rent reduction. As the value of land is closely connected with the amount of rent that the landlords are able to command, the reduction of rent in Taiwan should have the effect of an immediate decline in the value of farmland leased to tenant farmers. The Chinese Research Institute of Land Economics discovered, after a survey of farm values, that the average price of paddy fields of Taiwan dropped 19.4 per cent between December, 1948, and December, 1949, and that of dry land by 42.3 per cent in the same period. The decline was greater in the western part of the island than in the eastern part and greater in respect to land of higher grades than of lower grades because the original rent had been higher in the western part and in respect to land of higher grades. Therefore, when the ceiling of 37.5 per cent of rent was imposed on all farmland, the amount of rent actually reduced was larger for land of higher rent prior to reduction. According to the *Findings of the Cabinet Rent Reduction Inspection Team,* the average decline in the value of tenanted land in various counties and municipalities after rent reduction was from one third to one half, as compared with the period before rent reduction. For example,1 chia(0.9699 hectare or 2.3968 acres) of high grade (ninth) paddy field in Taitung Hsien was worth 23,880 kilograms (52,646 pounds) of unhulled rice in 1948. The price declined to 18,480 kilograms (40,741 pounds) in 1949 and still further to 10,920 kilograms (24,075 pounds) in 1950. Taking the price of 1948 as the base 100, the corresponding index is 77.4 in 1949 and 45.7 in 1950.[9] The value of land declined steadily after rent reduction, as is shown in Table 9.

But the decline was much more precipitous for leased land than for owner-cultivated land. For example, the value of owner-cultivated paddy fields of the fourth grade in Changhwa Hsien was approximately NT$12,000 (NT$ represents new Taiwan dollars) per chia while the leased paddy field of the same grade was only NT$ 7,000.[10] Similarly, 1 chia of owner-cultivated field of tenth grade was around NT$ 7,000, but 1 chia of leased paddy field of the same grade was only NT$ 4,000.[11] The differentials made absentee landowners suffer greater capital losses than did the owner-farmer, and certainly discouraged any future farmland speculators.

Table 9

Decline in the Value of Farmland After the 37.5 Per Cent
Rent Reduction

(Basic Period 1948 = 100)

Year	Seventh-Grade Paddy Field	Tenth-Grade Paddy Field	Sixteenth-Grade Paddy Field	Twenty-second-Grade Paddy Field
1948	100	100	100	100
49	65	71	67	65
50	67	63	57	41
51	56	48	42	38
52	38	43	35	27

Source: C. Cheng, *Land Reform in Taiwan* (Taipei: China Publishing Co., 1961), p. 310.

Following the land reform, it was anticipated that the increased income of the tenant farmers following rent reduction would result in an upward shift in their demand curve for land. But whether the reduced yield from the tenant farmland as a medium of investment would cause a shift to the right of the supply curve was not too obvious. Much would depend upon the yield from alternative forms of investment and the expectations as to any future action that the government would undertake with regard to tenant farmland. The very fact that the price of tenant land has fallen, and the number of tenant families purchasing land and the area of farmland purchased since the enforcement of rent reduction have increased,[12] shows that the supply and/ or demand curves of tenant farmland have presumably shifted to the right. Moreover, the extent of the shift is such as to cause the fall in the price of tenant farmland. It is of interest to note that most of the transactions (about 44 per cent of the total sales in the 1949–53 period) took place in 1953. This lends weight to the belief that the expectation of further government action was a more important factor in determining the shift of the supply curve because steps for implementing the land-to-the-tiller program were completed in February of that year and put immediately into effect. Landlords were anxious to sell their land in order to get the entire proceeds in cash. Such risk-aversion behavior of the landlords is understandable since they were afraid of any depreciation of the value of their money through an extended period of installment repayment.

SALE OF PUBLIC LAND

The second stage of the reform began with the sale of government land acquired after World War II from the Japanese nationals. When the island was under Japanese administration, land was set aside for Japanese immigrants. Japanese industrial firms and enterprises, such as the various sugar companies and Taiwan Colonization and Settlement Corporation, were large landlords. All this land, together with that owned by individual Japanese nationals and the various levels of government, was taken over by the Chinese Government in 1945 and thus became public farmland. It totaled 181,490 chia (434,981 acres), of which 74,198 chia (41 per cent) was paddy field and 107,292 chia (59 per cent) dry land.

The first attempt was to continue the old system of leasing the public land to the tenants, but rules were laid down to correct such malpractice as subleasing of land to tenant farmers for cultivation by those who were the lessees of the government. Farmers were encouraged to form cooperatives to lease the public land. The result of the leasing arrangement fell short of expectation on three counts: (1) The number of cooperatives formed did not come near to the expected figure because of lack of capital and equipment; (2) the configuration of the land was irregular; and (3) the members were unable to cooperate fully with one another in certain instances. Moreover, owing to the low rental rate, competition by individuals to lease public land was extremely keen. Complete fairness could hardly be expected in the parceling of the land or in the decision to lease any piece of land to one tenant instead of another.

The initial sale of public farmland to farmers was effected in 1948. It was designed to establish owner-farmers and to relieve rural unemployment through the reclamation of land, financed by the sale of public land. The project was temporarily suspended in 1949 and revived in 1951. The suspension was the result of the rent reduction program which led to the betterment of the farmers' livelihood and consequent disappearance of acute unemployment. But the need for help in establishing owner-farmers in Taiwan remained.

In June, 1951, the approval of the "Regulations Governing the Implementation of the Sale of Public Land to Help Establish Owner-Farmers in Taiwan" marked another milestone in land reform in Taiwan. The public land offered for sale was limited to that which was state-owned and province-owned. Of that, some was set aside chiefly for the Taiwan Sugar Corporation for the growth of sugar cane. Approximately 100,000 chia were made available for distribution, with preference given to the present tenant cultivators. The amount of public land which any one farm family was permitted to purchase was limited to 0.5 to 2 chia of paddy and 1 to 4 chia of dry land. The range in size of the land is necessary in order to account for the differences in the categories and grades of land in various parts of the island so that a reasonable level of living can be assured for the average farm family.

The correct appraisal of the land value is important to the success or failure of the program. The criterion adopted for the calculation of the land value was 2.5 times the annual main crop yield per chia of each grade of cultivated land. It was a good approximation of the market price of land, which was exactly 10 times the farm rent of the public land. The price units, being expressed in terms of farm products, were not subject to fluctuations in the value of the currency or changes in commodity price, and were easy for the farmers to understand.

The purchase price was paid in twenty, equal, semiannual installments which coincided with the harvest seasons (we will base our discussion on annual figures). As the land value was appraised at 2.5 times the total annual main crops, each of the annual installments would be 25 per cent of the total main crop yield. The land tax, which had to be paid together with the yearly installment payments, was approximately 7.5 per cent of the annual main crop yield in Taiwan and 4.5 per cent in Taipei for a paddy field of the thirteenth grade in 1953. With land tax added to the yearly installments, we arrive at a figure of 32.5 per cent of the standard amount of the total annual main crop yield as a maximum and 25.5 per cent as a minimum. Thus, the burden of the farmers who purchased public land would not be any higher than the tenant farmers who, after the enforcement of rent reduction, paid no more than 37.5 per cent of the annual main crop of the produce. All paddy fields had to be purchased with rice and all dry land with sweet potatoes, converted into monetary units according to the official rates.

The actual sale of public land in Taiwan took place by stages, and there were six successive sales from 1948 to 1958.

Some public land originally on the official list was removed as a result of field investigations. Some land had been washed away by floods; some was too poor in soil fertility or lacked proper irrigation facilities. Of the 181,490 chia (434,981 acres) of public land, the 71,666 chia (171,764 acres) sold to the farmers constituted a little over 39.5 per cent. A total of 139,688 families bought the 71,666 chia of land. The value of the land was 271,155 metric tons (298,897 short tons) of rice for paddy fields and 657,959 metric tons (725,174 short tons) of sweet potatoes for dry land. The average area purchased by each farming family was about 0.5 chia.[13] According to a Taiwan Land Bureau statistical study of farming familes that purchased public land under the sales program of 1948, 1951, and 1952, about 66 per cent purchased less than 0.5 chia (1.198 acres), 20 per cent purchased from 0.50 to 1 chia (from 1.198 to 2.397 acres), and less than 14 per cent purchased more than 1 chia. It is incorrect to conclude from these statistics that this was the only amount of land that they actually cultivated, as most purchasers cultivated other pieces of land. The total land actually cultivated by the farming families who bought public land under the sales program of 1948, 1951, and 1952 was 117,085 chia (280,620 acres). Of this, 50,622 chia (121,327 acres) was purchased from the government and the remaining 66,463 chia (159,293 acres) was either their own property or leased from others. Calculations made on the basis of these figures show that the average amount of land cultivated by each of those farming families that had purchased public land was 1.18 chia (2.83 acres). This average figure closely approximates the average amount of land (1.28 chia) cultivated by farming families throughout Taiwan during the period of 1950-52.

LAND-TO-THE-TILLER

The Land-to-the-Tiller Act was formally promulgated in 1953. Three basic ideas underlaid the act: (1) to help tenant farmers acquire landownership without increasing their financial burden; (2) to protect the interests of the landlords; and (3) to convert landholdings into industrial holdings. It was only natural that the present tenant cultivator should be given preference as the prospective buyer of the land compulsorily purchased and resold by the government. In addition, the farmers were permitted to pay for the land in installments over a ten-year period. The payments each farmer had to make in each of these years, including land tax, could not exceed the burden of 37.5 per cent of the annual main crops. A production fund was provided, from which loans at low rates of interest were extended. In addition, the farmers were provided with technical assistance in the form of modern farm technology.

The interest of the landlords was protected in two ways: First, the land that was compulsorily purchased was paid for at a reasonable price (which will be documented in Chapter 4). To safeguard their livelihood during the transition period of land occupation changes, provision was made for the retention of 3 chia of medium-grade land by individual landlords. Small landlords whose holdings did not exceed the retention limit might have their land exempted from compulsory purchase. To make profitable use of the money paid to them for the land, landlords were encouraged to invest in industrial development, converting their landholdings into industrial holdings. Measures were taken to transfer state-owned corporations to private ownership by offering the government stock for sale to private investors. Proceeds were used to pay for land compulsorily purchased from landlords.

In implementing the land-to-the-tiller program in Taiwan, investigation of land to be compulsorily purchased was an elaborate procedure, as was the resale. Interesting as they are from the viewpoint of public administration, we shall center our attention on the collection of the purchase price from farmer purchasers in this chapter and compensation to landlords in the following chapter.

The price of farmland offered by the government for resale was calculated on the same basis as that of farmland compulsorily purchased from landlords, namely, 2.5 times the total amount of its annual main crop yield for the respective land grades. Beginning with the season in which the land was purchased, the purchaser paid the price of the land plus 4 per cent interest per annum in twenty equal installments over a ten-year period, either in kind or in land bonds redeemable in kind. Payments in rice were delivered to the local warehouses designated by the Provincial Food Bureau, and payments in cash to the local branches of the Taiwan Land Bank. The rate at which rice and sweet potatoes were converted into cash was decided on the basis of the average wholesale quotations in important rice-producing townships. The total value of land, including immovable fixtures, resold as of June, 1954, by the government, together with interest thereon, was 1,528,000 metric tons of unhulled rice for the paddy fields and 522,365 metric tons of sweet potatoes for the dry land.[14]

In order to ensure the payment of principal and interest on the land bonds, a Land Bank Redemption Guaranty Fund was set up in addition to the general guarantee assumed by the Taiwan Provincial Treasury. The chief aim was that the fund might be used for making payments to landlords in case there should be a postponement or default in the installment payments by the land purchasers, or when they were exempted from making such payments owing to crop failure or other causes.

The completion of the successive stages of land reform has increased the area of farmland under the cultivation of owner-farmers. By area, 55 per cent of the farmland belonged to owner-cultivators in 1948. The percentage increased steadily over the years and became 82.9 per cent in 1953, 84.9 per cent in 1956 and 85.6 per cent in 1959.[15] A more dramatic way to picture the situation is to show the percentage of owner-farmers before and after the land reform. In Table 10 we find 57 per cent of the farm families were owner-cultivators in 1948 and that the percentage was 81 per cent in 1959—a remarkable change in slightly over a decade.

Table 10
Percentage Distribution of Farming Families
by Tenure for Selected Years

Year	(1) Owner-Cultivator	(2) Part-Owner	(3) Tenant Farmer	(4) Farm-hand	(5) (1)+(2)	(6) (3)+(4)
1948	33.02	24.10	36.08	6.80	57.12	42.88
1953	51.79	22.79	19.82	5.60	74.58	25.42
1956	57.05	22.10	15.86	5.00	79.15	20.86
1959	58.53	22.23	14.51	4.70	80.76	19.21

Source: C. Cheng, *Land Reform in Taiwan*   (Taipei: China Publishing Co., 1961), p. 312.

Along with the wider distribution of landownership, there was a reduction in the size of the holdings. Data are available only for selected years.[16] Ten per cent of the 1952 landholdings were below 0.5 hectare and 15 per cent between 0.5–0.99 hectare. In 1955 the corresponding percentage figures were 14 and 21, respectively. To summarize the pattern, 25 per cent of the landholdings in 1952 were below 1.0 hectare, while in 1955, the figure was 35 per cent.

Fragmentation of the landholdings in Taiwan, however, has been continuous for some time. In 1921, only 15 per cent of the landholdings were below 0.9699 hectare (1.0 chia); three decades went by before the percentage reached 25 per cent in 1952. But with the help of land reform, the same 10 per cent increase took place in landholdings below the 0.9699 hectare category in only three years.[17] It is common for holdings to be divided among several cultivators. The picture on land fragmentation is incomplete without looking further into the distribution of the number of cultivator families according to holding size. Table 11 gives the percentage distribution of cultivator families by size of farms. A large number of the farms classified by cultivator families were, in 1921 and the mid-1950's, of small sizes, namely, in class intervals below 0.5 chia and between 0.5–0.99 chia. Over a span of thirty-five years, 1921–56, there was remarkable stability in the distribution of the number of cultivator families. It was 30 per cent in both 1921 and 1956 in the class interval below 0.5 chia, with only a 5 to 6 per cent dip in intermediate years. In the next interval, 0.5–0.99 chia, we witness a 4 per cent increase between 1921 and 1956. One major difference between the patterns of distribution is at the high end. It was 0 per cent in 1956 for the number of cultivator families with 10 chia and over, whereas it was 1 per cent in 1921, 1932, and 1939. For cultivator families of 3 chia and above, the difference between 1956 and all other years is significant—7 per cent in 1956 and 13 to 16 per cent for the other years in the table.

Farm size in the long run is determined by farm area and the number of farm households. For the 1900-1960 period, the net gain in arable land used by agriculture was 320,000 hectares, a 60 per cent gain.[18] The gross increase was larger, but some arable land was lost yearly to nonagricultural uses. The more than 100 per cent increase in farm households between 1900 and 1960 is attributable to many factors, such as the increase in population, for example. More direct factors are the relative security of agricultural incomes and lack of investment opportunities in industrial and service sectors. Any biological and technological improvements, such as improved rice varieties,

Table 11
Number of Cultivator Families by Percentage
for Selected Years

Holding Size (chia)	1921	1932	1939	1956*
Below 0.5	30	25	26	30
0.5–0.99	23	20	20	27
1.0–3.99	34	39	39	36
3.0–9.99	12	15	14	7
10.0 and over	1	1	1	—
	100	100	100	100

* *Report on the 1956 Sample Census of Agriculture.*

Source: All figures are taken from *Statistical Abstract of Taiwan Province During the Fifty-one-Year Period* (in Chinese) (Taipei, 1946), except indicated otherwise.

irrigation, and greater use of commercial fertilizers, led to increased net farm incomes, which in turn attracted people into farming. The pull gets especially strong in an economy with population pressure and lagging industrial development. Thus, when discussing the impact of the declining farm size on agricultural productivity in Chapter 5, it will be important to keep in mind the distinction between the short- and long-run problems. In the long-run population pressure, lack of alternative opportunities in the industrial sector can only be remedied by industrial development or a check on too rapid a rate of population expansion, or both. It is a problem of a different order of magnitude. In the short run, excessive division of farm lots into smaller units may be corrected by land consolidation, to which we now turn.

REDEMARCATION OF LAND

The redemarcation of land in Taiwan is a part of the land reform program aimed at bringing about a more economical utilization of land in order to achieve the goal of reducing production costs and increasing yields. Even after the land-to-the-tiller program, factors still exist that prevent the full development of the land potential. They are: (1) poor drainage and inadequate irrigation; (2) undesirable division of farm lots in irregular shapes; (3) dispersal of farmland owned by the same farmer; and (4) shortage of good farm roads for transporting fertilizers, produce, farm machinery, and equipment.

The land redemarcation project was carried out in stages. Several areas in central Taiwan were heavily devastated by the flood of August 7, 1959. In the postflood rehabilitation program, efforts were directed not only to reclaim the land but also to its redemarcation, to insure more efficient utilization. Only when the farmland was of 50 hectares or more and when owners were not able to resume farming activities by themselves, was the land redemarcated. A total of 817 hectares of flooded farmland in nine different *hsiens* was redemarcated.[19]

Gratifying results of the redemarcation of flooded land led to the subsequent decision that the program should be carried out on a much wider scale. As a preparatory step to the implementation of a long-term, continuing project, a demonstration redemarcation of farmland was put into effect in 1961. Because of seasonal factors in seeding and harvesting various crops on the farm, the timing of the implementation is of crucial importance to the success of the project. For example, the ideal time for redemarcation of the double-crop paddy land is between the end of November to February of the following year. For single-crop field, it is between April and June. Attention to such details made the project acceptable to more than 98 per cent of the landowners of the eleven affected districts. A total of 3,362 hectares of farmland was redemarcated. The details of the achievement are reflected by the following comparison. First, there is a net increase in the producing area of 4.47 per cent. Second, 81 per cent of the lots are concentrated in one place and 14 per cent at two sites, as compared with 40 per cent and 35 per cent, respectively, before the consolidation. Third, land with direct drainage and irrigation has increased more than threefold. The success of these two projects has led to voluntary requests by farmers in many other districts for redemarcation of their land.[20]

The immediate benefit of the project can be expressed in terms of increased land productivity. According to the reports of several districts, such as Yunlin, Taichung, and Changhwa, the rice productivity has been increased by 25 per cent. The following are the contributing factors: First, accessibility of farms to roads enables farmers to increase use of organic fertilizers from compost piles by as much as 3 to 5 times. Second, better irrigation and drainage facilities make control of water in the field feasible, thus increasing the efficiency of the fertilizers and decreasing the loss of crops through poor drainage. Third, consolidation of scattered pieces of land not only increases the production area but also makes possible deep plowing by farm machinery.

SUMMARY AND CONCLUSION

This chapter presented the highlights of the land reform: (1) the rent reduction and improvement of tenancy terms; (2) the sale of public land; and (3) the land-to-the-tiller program, under which absentee landlords were forced to sell their land in excess of certain maximum holdings.

The immediate consequence of these measures was an increase in the number of owner-cultivators and greater concentration of landholdings in units of less than 1.0 chia, although the fragmentation of landholdings was held somewhat in check by land redemarcation. But the long-run impact of land reform on the size of landholdings is difficult to determine. It is true that for a given holding the increase of land productivity tends to draw more people to the farm if job opportunities in the other sectors are not available or attractive enough. But one must not overlook what land reform has done in raising the income of the farmers (Chapter 4), which, in turn, places education within reach of those who normally could not have afforded it (Chapter 7). The contribution of the education and training of rural children to out-migration from the farm and to reducing the need for a large stock of capital for industrial production, by perhaps acting as a substitute for it, is yet to be discussed. We mention these considerations here to prevent any unqualified generalization based only on the experience of the years immediately following the land reform.

4

CHANGES IN RELATIVE INCOME POSITION

Of the many consequences of land reform, two immediate effects on income change deserve our attention. One is compensation to landlords for land sold under the land-to-the-tiller program and the other is the changing income of the tenants and the new owner-cultivators as a result of rent reduction. Our focus in the present chapter will be on the primary effects. The secondary increase of their income, following the rise of agricultural productivity, will only be referred to in passing. The broader issue of the relationship between land reform and yield will be examined in Chapter 5.

COMPENSATION TO EX-LANDLORDS

For the land sold under the land-to-the-tiller program, landlords were paid 2.5 times the annual yield, as mentioned in the previous chapter. It is true that paddy farms commanded a price between 3 and 4 times the annual yield prior to land reform.[1] However, with reduced rent goes the lower land price, so valuation at 2.5 times the annual yield seems to have been in line with the return of investment in farmland and to have reflected the market valuation.[2] In other words, whatever capital loss was sustained was at the initiation of rent reduction rather than at that of the land-to-the-tiller program.

Of the total compensation, landlords were paid 70 per cent in land bonds in kind and 30 per cent in government enterprise stocks. There are two kinds of land bonds: rice bonds and sweet potato bonds, both bearing an annual interest of 4 per cent. Compensation for paddy fields was paid with rice bonds and for dry land, with sweet potato bonds. Approximate adjustments were made for compensating double-crop, three-year rotation and specially irrigated fields.

In paying part of the compensation to landlords with government enterprise stocks, the quantity of rice or sweet potatoes that any given landlord was entitled to receive as compensation first had to be converted into monetary terms at the rate of NT$160 to 100 kilograms of unhulled rice and NT$38.85 to 100 kilograms of sweet potatoes. The conversion rates were based on the general average commodity price for Taiwan in December, 1952, as was the reevaluation of the assets of the government enterprises offered for sale.

The total area of farmland compulsorily purchased from landlords was 143,568 hectares, consisting mostly of paddy land (Table 12). Half of the landlords sold land of less than 1.0 hectare and about 17 per cent sold 3.0 hectares or more. In terms of farm area sold, those who sold 3.0 hectares or more contributed 40 per cent of the total paddy land and 45 per cent of the dry land. Paddy fields were valued at 1,272,855 metric tons of unhulled rice, and the dry land, including immovable fixtures, was valued at 434,709 metric tons of sweet potatoes. If converted into monetary terms, in accordance with respective market prices in December, 1952, this would be equivalent to NT$2,205,452,000.

For 30 per cent of the compensation for land compulsorily purchased, the government paid with its stocks in the Taiwan Cement Corporation, the Taiwan Paper and Pulp Corporation, the Taiwan Agricultural and Forestry Development Corporation, and the Taiwan Industrial and Mining Corporation. Each landlord had to take a bundle of all four stocks: 37 per cent of stocks in the Taiwan Cement Corporation, 33 per cent in the Taiwan Paper and Pulp Corporation, 13 per cent in the Taiwan Agricultural and Forestry, and the remaining 17 per cent in the Taiwan Forestry and Development Corporation. The total capital value of the four corporations was fixed at NT$970 million, which was divided into 97 million shares (with par value of NT$10 per share) of which 79,022,417 shares were owned by the state and province. The 30 per cent of land value to be paid to landlords, when converted into monetary terms (according to the average market values of rice and sweet potatoes for December, 1952, and calculated in terms of industrial stocks), was NT$660,292,420 or 84 per cent of the total value of government stocks. But as portions of a share were paid in cash, such cash payments accounted for NT$517,780. Consequently, the total value of government stocks actually transferred to landlords was only NT$659,774,640.[3]

Table 12
Distribution of Landlords by Size of Land Sold

Size (in hectares)	Number of Landlords Classified by Size of Land Sold	Farm Area Sold by Landlords (Hectares)		
		Paddy Land	Dry Land	Total
Less than 0.5	27,668 (26.08%)	11,582 (9.52%)	2,353 (10.67%)	13,935 (9.70%)
0.5—less than 1.0	24,519 (23.12)	19,142 (15.74)	3,012 (13.67)	22,154 (15.43)
1.0—less than 1.5	15,451 (14.56)	15,495 (12.74)	2,358 (10.70)	17,817 (12.41)
1.5—less than 2.0	9,757 (9.20)	11,534 (9.49)	1,813 (8.22)	13,347 (9.29)
2.0—less than 3.0	11,039 (10.40)	15,520 (12.76)	2,521 (11.44)	18,041 (12.56)
3.0—higher	17,615 (16.61)	48,298 (39.73)	9,976 (45.27)	58,274 (40.58)
Total	106.049 (100%)	121,535 (100%)	22,033 (100%)	143,568 (100%)

Source: Rural Economic Division, JCRR, 62–RED–M–165. Estimates of number of landlords where land was compulsorily purchased by the government are based on *Statistics on Landownership Classification in 1953* (Department of Civil Affairs, Taiwan Provincial Government).

How the four corporations were to be operated after their transfer to private ownership was a subject of much discussion and concern. Assurance was given by the government in October, 1954, that assistance would be maintained until the end of 1957 in the form of special facilities for short-term loans, allotment of the necessary amount of foreign exchange for the purchase of raw materials and equipment, government assistance in the improvement and expansion of productive installations, etc. Despite such promises of assistance, the ex-landlords had little interest in holding on to the stocks they received.

A classic example of a large landlord who transferred his financial resources from farmland to the industrial enterprises is the present major stockholder of the Taiwan Cement Corporation. More significant for our study is what happened to the disposition of funds paid as compensation to the majority of the ex-landlords. The Rural Economics and Farmer's Organization Division of the Sino-American Joint Commission on Rural Reconstruction (JCRR) has conducted interviews with the ex-landlords. Twenty-four families (including small, medium, and large landlords mostly on the western part of the island) were convered. [4] It shows that in the sample of twenty-four landholders, between 70 to 80 per cent of their land was sold, depending upon whether they were small or large landlords. The over-all picture of the interview clearly points to their preference for land bonds over industrial stocks as a medium of investment. Of the four industrial stocks, the Taiwan Cement Corporation stock was preferred over the other three. Of the thirteen small landholders, three sold their land bonds and nine or ten sold all or part of their industrial shares. Only one medium landholder sold the land bond and five disposed of all or part of the industrial shares. Of the large landholders, none sold their land bonds, but all had liquidated a part or all of the industrial shares. [5]

The reasons given for their decisions are of interest. The ex-landlords had little knowledge of or experience in owning or managing an enterprise. The fluctuation of the market price of their shares was to them a source of uncertainty, especially when the market price went below the par value of the stocks, as was the case for all industrial stocks except those of the Cement Corporation.

Since a sample of twenty-four ex-landlords out of a population of 106,149 is much too small, and there is no other direct evidence, we need some additional indication of their investment behavior. The stocks of the Taiwan Cement Corporation seem to have been retained by a larger fraction of the original stockholders. The three other corporations either disposed of or reorganized the original units in the corporate structure after having been turned over to the private owners, and it is difficult to retrace the ex-landlord proportion of the existing stockholders.

Our search and result were based on matching the list of stockholders of the Cement Corporation and the number of hectares sold by the landlords, classified by size. The details of our estimation procedure, though interesting, are relegated to the footnote.[6] However, from our analysis, the retention of shares by the original landlords seems to be low. It is especially true of the small landlords (only 4.5 per cent of shares issued to the landlords who sold less than 0.5 hectare of paddy land were retained). This shows that the small landlords preferred to make use of their money in ways other than industrial stockholdings. The percentage of retention seemed to move up steadily with each class interval. The retention rate was 9.3 per cent for those who sold land between 2 to 3 hectares.

Some landlords also did not have confidence in the bonds, as reflected in the pattern of bond market prices which were much below the face value. As each installment was met by the government, confidence improved and the bond price remained about the same in spite of the fact that part of the principal was paid off after each installment date. Undoubtedly, losses were taken by those who disposed of the bonds before maturity date. But the great majority of ex-landlords held on to their bonds and found them a rewarding investment medium.

INCOME OF TENANTS AND CULTIVATOR-PURCHASERS

we shall begin the estimation of the income derived by the farmers as a result of the reshaping of agrarian institutions at the micro level, i.e., based on the tenant farmers' paddy and brown-rice production per hectare. We shall take 1948, before the implementation of the land reform, as the base year. According to one estimate given by the Taiwan Provincial Food Bureau[7] to illustrate the increase in income to tenants after land reform, the 1948 production (on a two crops a year basis) was 3,894 kilograms per hectare. This figure, though lower than the one shown by the Bureau of Land at their exhibit commemorating the tenth anniversary of the land-to-the-tiller program in May, 1963, in Taipei, was much higher than the national average of 3,104 kilograms per hectare for paddy field and even higher than the average yield for Ponlai rice, which generally gives the highest yield. We do not have here a problem of deciding on a figure that is more representative. For our present purpose, we shall go through all three sets of calculations, but only the one given by the Taiwan

Provincial Food Bureau is presented in Table 13. Because of price changes, we follow the practice of expressing the costs and receipts in units of kilograms of rice. In Table 13, the rent before land reform in 1948 is estimated to be 50 per cent of the output per hectare on paddy field, or 50 per cent x 3,894 kilograms - 1,947 kilograms. Fertilizer cost is estimated to be 118 kilograms per hectare. This left the tenant farmer with a residual of 1,829 kilograms per hectare to cover other costs of rice production, including the reward for his services. For 1949 and thereafter, a figure of 37.5 per cent of the 1948 output is used for calculating the rent because of the implementation of the rent limitation, i.e., 1,460 kilograms (37.5 per cent x 3,894). As long as the land was not upgraded, the rent payment remained fixed at 1,460 kilograms per hectare per annum.

Column 1 of Table 13 records the rice production in 1948-60 based on two crops of paddy rice. Column 2 records the quantity of paddy rice bartered for fertilizer, which goes up year after year. The trend represents an increasingly larger use of fertilizer than the figures in the columns indicate because the barter ratio between chemical fertilizer and rice actually declined in terms of rice since 1949.[8] The figures in Column 3 represent the gross receipt of the farmers after deducting the costs of fertilizer. In 1949, for example, the output for two crops of paddy was 4,248 kilograms of rice, from which we subtract 388 kilograms for fertilizer to get the gross receipt of 3,860 kilograms in Column 3. Column 4 reflects the increase of production over the base year, 1948. Column 5 shows the difference in fertilizer application between the figures for 1948 and the corresponding ones in subsequent years. Again we refer to the specific figures for 1949 as an illustration. The difference between the production in 1949 and 1948 is 354 kilograms of rice (Column 4) and the difference in the use of fertilizer is 270 kilograms of rice. The figures in Column 6 are the difference between the corresponding figures in Columns 4 and 5. The difference represents the increase in income to the farmers on account of the increase in yield. The total increment of income to the farmers after the implementation of the 37.5 per cent land rent limitation program is shown in Column 14, which consists of two parts: increase caused by rent reduction, i.e., 487 kilograms (the difference between 1,947 kilograms and 1,460 kilograms in Column 10), and net increase in yield (Column 6). Comparing the figures in Column 14, we find 571 kilograms in 1949 and 1,957 kilograms in 1960, or a rise of about 340 per cent in a short span of eleven years.[9]

Table 13
Estimated Increase of Income Derived from Rent Limitation
by Tenant Farmers (Based on Paddy-Rice Production per Hectare)
(Unit: Kilograms of Paddy-Rice)

				Income for Production Increase		
	(1)	(2)	(3)	(4)	(5)	(6)
	Production (2 Crops of Paddy Rice)	Quantity of Paddy Rice Bartered for Fertilizer	Gross Receipt (1) - (2)	Increase of Production over 1948	Increase of Paddy Rice for Fertilizer over 1948	Net (4)-(5)
Before 37.5 per cent rent limitation:						
1948	3894	118	3776			
After 37.5 per cent rent limitation:						
1949	4248	388	3860	354	270	84
1950	4822	608	4214	928	490	438
1951	4916	681	4235	1022	563	459
1952	5216	801	4415	1322	683	639
1953	5388	805	4583	1494	687	807
1954	5562	977	4585	1668	859	809
1955	5472	1010	4462	1578	892	686
1956	5786	1052	4734	1892	934	958
1957	5968	1074	4894	2074	956	1118
1958	6174	1111	5063	2280	993	1287
1959	6062	1110	4952	2168	992	1176
1960	6366	1120	5246	2472	1002	1470

Source: (1). *Food Production and Activities of the Taiwan Provincial Food Bureau* (Taiwan Provincial Food Bureau, 1962), p. 41.

(2). *Ibid.*

(3). (1) - (2).

(4). Calculated from (1).

(5). Calculated from (2).

(6). (4) - (5).

	Alternative Rent System			Net Increase of Income from Change of Rent and Productivity Since Base Year, 1948			
(7) 50 Per Cent of Yield (Current Year)	(8) 37.5 Per Cent of Yield (Current Year)	(9) 50 Per Cent of Yield (Base Year, 1948)	(10) 37.5 Per Cent of Yield (Base Year, 1948)	(11) Under Rent of (7)	(12) Under Rent of (8)	(13) Under Rent of (9)	(14) Under Rent of (10)
1947		1947		1829		1829	
2124	1593	1947	1460	-93	438	84	571
2411	1808	1947	1460	-26	577	438	925
2458	1844	1947	1460	-52	567	459	946
2608	1956	1947	1460	-22	630	639	1126
2694	2021	1947	1460	60	733	807	1294
2781	2086	1947	1460	-25	670	809	1296
2736	2052	1947	1460	-103	581	686	1173
2893	2170	1947	1460	12	735	958	1445
2984	2238	1947	1460	81	827	1118	1605
3087	2315	1947	1460	147	919	1287	1774
3031	2273	1947	1460	92	850	1176	1663
3183	2387	1947	1460	234	1030	1470	1957

(7), (8), (9), and (10). Calculated from (1).

(11). (6) + 1947 kg. - (7).

(12). (6) + 1947 kg. - (8).

(13). (6) + 1947 kg. - (9).

(14). (6) + 1947 kg. - (10).

Attention should be drawn to the components of the total increase of income. In the years immediately following the land rent limitation, total increase of income to the tenant farmers consisted largely of reduced rent. In the later years, as the farmers applied more fertilizer, and possibly more labor, to the land, the increase of output as a part of gains became much more pronounced. The figures in Table 13 are an example. In 1949, out of the total increase of income of 571 kilograms per hectare, 487 kilograms, or 85 per cent, came from reduced rent; in 1960, the proportion is reduced to 24 per cent (i.e., 487/1957).

So far we have confined ourselves to a calculation of the increase in income based on one form of the rent reduction program. To see the impact on income redistribution under alternative forms of rent collections (Columns 7, 8, and 9), we have made calculations in Columns 11, 12, and 13 for the purpose of comparing the gains to the tenants. For example, suppose that the original rate system was 50 per cent of the output of the current year, as shown in Column 7 of Table 13. Then, when the yield increases, the rent payment will increase proportionately (Column 7), i.e., 50 per cent of the increase of the yield will go to the landlord as rent. However, rent limitation can mean a reduction of the percentage from, say, 50 per cent to 37.5 per cent, but rent will still be calculated on the current yield basis. Although the annual new rent will be less than the old rate of 50 per cent, it is still proportional to the productivity, as shown in Column 8. The second type of rent limitation is to designate the output of one year as the base for calculating rent independent of the output of the current year. Referring to the previous example in Table 13, we find that if 1948 were chosen as the base year, 50 per cent rent would result in 1,947 kilograms rent (Column 9) and 37.5 per cent in 1,460 kilograms rent (Column 10). The net revenues to the tenants under various rent systems are depicted in Figure 1.

Curves A and C represent the increase in income from 1948 if the rent were assessed on 37.5 per cent and 50 per cent, respectively, of the 1948 base-year yield. Naturally, A is above C every year by a fixed distance of 487 kilograms, i.e., 12.5 per cent multiplied by the base-year yield. Curves B and D represent the increase in income from 1948 if the rent were assessed at 37.5 per cent and 50 per cent, respectively, of the actual yield of each year. Most portions of D lie below the base line, indicating a net reduction in income because of the higher costs of fertilizer not covered by the higher yield. There is no doubt

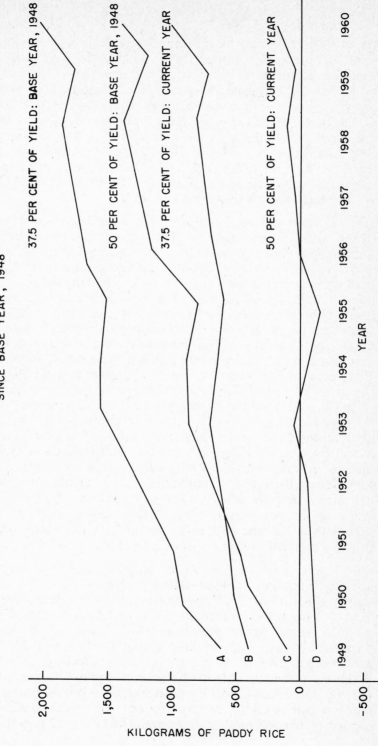

FIGURE I

NET INCREASE OF INCOME FROM CHANGES IN RENT AND PRODUCTIVITY
SINCE BASE YEAR, 1948

37.5 PER CENT OF YIELD: BASE YEAR, 1948

50 PER CENT OF YIELD: BASE YEAR, 1948

37.5 PER CENT OF YIELD: CURRENT YEAR

50 PER CENT OF YIELD: CURRENT YEAR

that tenants fared best under the 37.5 per cent fixed-base rent scheme (or worst from the landlord's point), which is the one actually adopted, since curve A is everywhere above B, C, or D. The relative position of B and C are worth noting. In the three years immediately following 1948, B stays above C. In other words, a high fixed rent may indeed make the tenant worse off than a lower rate based on the actual yield. It is only when the increase in yield is sufficiently high, as was the case in Taiwan after 1953, that the 50 per cent rent based on the 1948 yield made the tenants better off than a 37.5 per cent rent calculated on the actual yield.

We next turn our attention to the land-to-the-tiller program which was implemented in 1953. The increase of income to the farmer-purchasers will be estimated in Table 14, and we shall use the same sets of production and cost of fertilizer figures (Columns 1 and 3) as employed in evaluating the increase in income from the 37.5 per cent rent reduction. The new items that require explanation are taxes and land cost repayment. Since the tenant purchasers became owners, they now pay land taxes, but not rent. The land tax expressed in terms of rice amounted to 229 kilograms per hectare, as shown in Table 14. The repayment cost of land is expressed as 30 per cent of the yield in 1948. The method of calculating the repayment cost is explained in the footnote.[10] Again, the figure in Table 14 is an illustration. The output per hectare in 1948 was 3,894 kilograms and land cost repayment is 30 per cent of the 1948 output (2 crops), or 1,168 kilograms. The figures in Column 2 are output minus tax (229 kilograms). After deducting the cost of fertilizers (Column 3) from the figures in Column 2, we have the net farm income of the farmers (Column 4), from which they pay the annual installment on land cost. Column 6 gives the disposable income of the farmers, i.e., net income (Column 4) minus repayment cost (Column 5).

There are two ways of looking at the changing income aspect of the land-to-the-tiller program. One is to examine the disposable income of the farmers before and after the purchase. The tenant farmers paid an annual rent of 1,460 kilograms before their purchase (Table 14). When they became owner-cultivators, they paid instead the land tax (229 kilograms) and repayment cost (1,168 kilograms), totaling 1,397 kilograms. When we compare this with the rent payment, the owner-cultivators were better off by 63 kilograms per hectare. However, the income used to defray the cost of land repayment has the nature of forced saving and cannot be lumped together with the

Table 14

Estimated Increase of Income Derived by
Farmers After Land-to-the-Tiller
(Based on the Rice Production per Hectare in One Whole Year)

Year	(1) Production (2 Crops of Paddy Rice)	(2) Gross (After Tax = 229 kilograms)	(3) Quantity of Paddy Rice Bartered for Fertilizer	(4) Net Farm Income	(5) Land Cost Repayment (3894 x 30 per cent)	(6) Dis- posable Income
1953	5,388	5,159	805	4,354	1,168	3,186
1954	5,562	5,333	977	4,356	1,168	3,188
1955	5,472	5,243	1,010	4,233	1,168	3,065
1956	5,786	5,557	1,052	4,505	1,168	3,337
1957	5,968	5,339	1,074	4,265	1,168	3,097
1958	6,174	5,945	1,111	4,834	1,168	3,666
1959	6,062	5,833	1,110	4,723	1,168	3,555
1960	6,366	6,137	1,120	5,017	1,168	3,849

Comparison of Disposable Income:
(1) Tenant after land rent limitation: rent   1460
(2) Owner-cultivator after land-to-the-tiller:
    tax and repayment cost   1397
                                         63

Comparison of Net Receipt:
(1) Tenant after land rent limitation: rent   1460
(2) Owner-cultivator after land-to-the-tiller:
    tax   229
                                    1231

Source: Same as Table 13.

land tax. To account for this, we take the net figure between the rent and the land tax as an indication of the change of the financial status of the tenants after becoming owner-cultivators. In Table 14, we arrive at a net addition of 1,231 kilograms per hectare (1,460 kilograms minus 229 kilograms).[11] Even by comparing disposable income, the owner-cultivators fared slightly better or about the same as the tenant. An uncertain element in this comparison is the tax rate. The risk of a rising tax rate is borne by the owner, but not by the tenant. If the tax rate is as fixed as the rent, land purchase obviously becomes attractive to the owner-cultivators.

It is noteworthy that the estimated increase of income to the farmers is largely attributable to the increase of rice productivity in recent years. As a check on the reliability of the increase we examine the per capita consumption of rice and other staples (wheat flour and sweet potatoes) in the 1950's, based on JCRR estimate of total rice consumption in Taiwan. The consumption figure was derived by deducting the amount exported and used for other purposes (including changes in government rice inventory) from the official estimates of rice production.[12] It was found that the rice consumption figure per head since 1955, particularly 1959 and 1960, has been generally on a higher level than in the early years. Under the situation of rising income, one would normally expect a steady per capita increase of fish and pork consumption as is indeed true in Taiwan. However, we do not find a gradual decline of the consumption of rice and other staples, but a concomitant increase. Since it is not likely that the statistics on rice exports and inventory contain errors, one suspects that the official estimates of rice production in recent years may have been on the high side.[13]

INCOME, SAVING, AND CONSUMPTION IN THE AGRICULTURAL SECTOR

Detailed statistics on agricultural income, consumption, and saving are available for the years 1950, 1955, and 1960, thus giving us an opportunity to examine the impact of land reform as shown in aggregate statistics. Data collected for 1950 (one year after rent reduction) are considered to reflect the conditions prior to land reform; data collected for 1955 reflect conditions at the mid-point; and by 1960, the immediate impact of the land reform should have been fully eliminated. To facilitate comparison, we have converted all items in terms of the 1934-37 Taiwan dollar. In 1950, the flow of farm income to the sectors outside agriculture in the form of land rent, interest charges, and taxes was higher in percentage (30 per cent) than in 1955 (18 per cent); the downward trend continued into 1960 (11 per cent), as shown in Table 15. One of the major items that caused the large outflow was the land rent. The distribution of income inside the farm sector also saw a substantial increase of

Table 15

Flow of Net Farm Income Outside and Inside the Farm Sector for Selected Years
(in 1935-37 Taiwan Dollars)

	1950		1955		1960*	
	T$1000	Per Cent	T$1000	Per Cent	T$1000	Per Cent
Flow of Farm Income to Outside Sectors	92,877	30.48	71,062	17.86	48,127	10.69
Land rent paid	62,624	20.55	23,950	6.02	16,790	3.73
Interest paid	11,304	3.71	13,766	3.46	6,833	1.52
Taxes paid	18,949	6.22	33,346	8.38	24,504	5.44
Flow of Farm Income Inside Farm Sector	211,858	69.52	326,777	82.14	402,224	89.32
Wage payment	118,767	38.97	191,077	48.03	236,504	52.52
Rent for farmers' own land	69,325	22.75		24.42	97,174	21.58
Interest for farmers' own capital	23,766	7.80		9.69	68,546	15.22
Total Net Farm Income	304,735	100.00	397.837	100.00	450,352	100.00
Total Gross Farm Income	471,091		535,872		643,791	

* JCRR data.

Source: H. S. Tang and S. C. Hsieh, "Land Reform and Agricultural Development in Taiwan" in Walter Froehlich (ed.), *Land Tenure Industrialization and Social Stability* (Milwaukee: Marquette University Press, 1961), p. 130.

wage payments and concomitant reduction of implicit rent in 1955 and 1960, as compared with 1950. The rise in wage payments was largely due to including the owners' own wages, since much of the land was owned by the farmers themselves within the sector.

To throw further light on the extent of income change before and after land reform, it is necessary to compare absolute figures and calculate their percentage changes over the years. A note of caution should be sounded in such a comparison, as it was in discussing rice yield. Estimates of Taiwan's gross national product (GNP) and national income for the 1950's are under review by the government. The actual rate of growth was probably in the neighborhood of 7 to 7.5 per cent, which is lower than the official estimate of 8 per cent.

We shall, therefore, tentatively adopt 1 per cent per annum as the correcting factor. Accordingly, we have reduced the gross farm income in 1955 by 5 per cent, i.e., from T$536 million to T$509 million, and the gross farm incomes in 1960 by 10 per cent, i.e., from $644 million to $579 million.[14] Expressing the difference of two, successive, five-year periods by means of per cent, we find an 8 per cent increase in gross farm income during the period of 1950-55 and a 14 per cent increase during 1955-60.

As a further check on the reliability of these figures in reflecting economic reality, we compare the percentage increase in rice yield for the same two, successive, five-year periods (Table 13) and find an increase of 13.5 per cent and 11.7 per cent, respectively, after having made the appropriate adjustment of the yield figure for 1960 to make our comparison meaningful.[15]

By cross-checking the rice yield with the gross farm income, we have a picture of income change in the farm sector after the land reform. Rise in rice yield led the farm economy in income increase in the first five-year period, but the lead was taken over by a more rapid rise of nonfarm income in the second five-year period.

Statistics on farm-family income, consumption, and saving with subtotals from farm and nonfarm sources in Table 16 make possible a verification of the picture just painted. Taking

Table 16

Income, Consumption, and Saving of the Farm Sector for Selected Years
(in 1935-37 Taiwan Dollars)

	1950		1955		1960*	
	T$1000	Per Cent	T$1000	Per Cent	T$1000	Per Cent
Retained net farm income (farm earnings)	211,858	76.62	326,777	86.47	402,224	69.75
Nonfarm income	64,860	23.28	51,112	13.53	174,416	30.25
Total farm family income	276,718	100.0	377,899	100.00	576,640	100.00
Total consumption	238,973	85.77	339,109	89.74	482,813	83.73
Farm products	119,384	42.85	152,599	40.38	230,121	39.91
Nonfarm products	119,589	42.92	186,520	49.36	252,692	43.82
Total saving	39,567	14.20	38,476	10.88	92,712	16.08
Agricultural investment	36,454	13.08	30,543	8.08	84,333	14.63
Nonagricultural investment	3,113	1.12	7,933	2.10	8,379	1.45
Statistical discrepency	86	0.03	304	0.08	1,115	0.19

* JCRR data.

Source: H. S. Tang and S. C. Hsieh, "Land Reform and Agriculture Development in Taiwan" in Walter Froehlich (ed.), *Land Tenure Industrialization and Social Stability* (Milwaukee: Marquette University Press, 1961), p. 131.

the period of 1950-60 as a whole, the nonfarm income appears to have become more important. The nonfarm income in 1950 was 23 per cent of total farm-family income. This per cent declined between 1950 and 1955, and increased between 1955 and 1960. This might mean that the short-run effect of land reform was to depress the nonfarm share of farm income. A priori, one would certainly expect this. The dramatic change took place in 1955-60. In 1955, nonfarm income was only 14 per cent of the total farm-family income; in 1960, it was 30 per cent—a more than 100 per cent increase in absolute as well as relative terms.

The impact of increase in farm income and consumption in the nonagricultural sectors will be discussed in Chapter 8.

Another figure of interest is the per cent of income saved in the farm sector. On account of the implementation of the land-to-the-tiller program, with its consequent greater equality in income distribution in the farm sector, we are interested in comparing the per cent of income saved in the farm sector for the period of 1950-60. Here we encounter the same problem of underestimation as the gross farm income discussed earlier. The sample survey of farm family expenditures included the cost of house maintenance, but not house rent. Since the farm houses in Taiwan are generally well built, the maintenance cost was not a true reflection of imputed rent. Another source of inaccuracy is the estimated expenditure on public utility services such as electricity and water. The estimation has been based on the same expenditures as for the urban families. But a significant fraction of the sample population consisted of government employees of public enterprises (government-owned and operated) who either enjoyed free services or paid for them at a nominal charge. In addition, it was discovered in the 1950-51 survey that rice farmers consumed much more rice than an average family. To lessen the bias, a flat percentage was applied to reduce the estimated consumption of the farm families. But such a procedure overlooks the fact that the consumption expenditure on items other than rice was not out of line to the same extent as the expenditure on rice. Since 1956, this downward bias has been modified to some extent because of the selection of relatively prosperous farm families in the sample, but the net effect of such a correction procedure is difficult to assess.

In view of underestimation of both gross farm income and consumption, the estimated saving is naturally under suspicion.

Since saving is estimated as a residual, i.e., the difference between two underestimated figures, the bias could be in either direction. No simple procedure can be improvised to make the necessary adjustment. Thus, the estimated savings in Table 16 stand unchanged and should be taken only as a rough indication of actual farm savings. This reservation applies equally to the ratio between saving and income in the table. We should certainly be on guard when using the estimated savings in our discussion of the flow of savings between the agricultural and nonagricultural sectors in Chapter 6 and when accepting the result therefrom.

SUMMARY AND CONCLUSION

Of total compensation to landlords, 70 per cent of land value was paid in rice and potato bonds, which are good inflation hedgers and guarantee a regular return. The other 30 per cent was paid in public-enterprise stocks, of which one third was in shares of the Taiwan Cement Corporation. The company has consistently maintained a satisfactory earning record and has greatly expanded. Of somewhat dubious value were the shares of the other three corporations which consisted of slightly less than 20 per cent of the total payment. The market prices of these shares suffered a decline, except for an occasional price recovery. Some experience in corporate management and stockhandling could have preserved most of the initial value, if not actually having realized a profit. But this type of experience may be too much to expect from the small ex-landlords. However, losses suffered in quick disposal of land bonds are quite unwarranted.

The sources of increased income to the tenants are rent limitation and increase in land productivity and total output by adding one or more crops. The part played by rent reduction was significant in the first few years following the land reform. Since rent was made a fixed charge by the land reform, it became a smaller fraction of the total cost as production increased with the years. It worked to the advantage of the tenant and owner-cultivator to have rent and land tax, respectively, set as a fixed charge. On an aggregate level, the rise of income, consumption, and saving of the farm sector during 1950-60 was substantial even after due allowance was made of a margin for possible error in such an estimation. Since the increase in rice yield was initially responsible for the main thrust, in Chapter 5 we shall examine the way and, if possible, the extent, to which land reform could and did contribute to this end.

CHAPTER 5 AGRICULTURAL PRODUCTIVITY

The discussion of the income effects accompanying land reform shows that the major portion of the rise of income stems from the increased productivity of the land. Aside from the question of the reliability of these figures, there is the more pertinent question of whether the growth of productivity has been caused by land reform. Students of land reform believe that there are conflicting forces working on the productivity of land after land reform. For example, there is the matter of incentives. It is argued that although one does not deny the adverse effects of a heavy rent on the efforts and incentives of tenants, it would be difficult to establish their general importance. Significantly, with lower rent there is a possibility of output reduction in the short run "if the tenants prefer to take out the windfall gain partly or wholly in the form of more leisure."[1]

The tendency toward fragmentation of farmland following the sale of public land and the land-to-the-tiller program is another issue in point. A farm is an economic unit, and there are economies of scale. The experience of United States agriculture points to the consolidation of small farms into the larger ones. Larger farms, as a rule, can compete more effectively for the factors of production and combine them more efficiently; they can also afford to use more specialized labor and equipment. On the other hand, if the size of the individual unit is small enough, the owner-cultivator is forced to apply more labor per unit of land, especially if he is restricted in outside earnings. He and his family would work until the marginal satisfaction derived from his income is equal to the marginal disutility of work; but since he has to achieve a minimum subsistence level of income, the marginal utility of income would be indeed very high.[2]

Consequently, no a priori generalization of the net effect is possible in view of the diversity of conditions in the underdeveloped countries and the differences in the levels of development attained in each. Our probing into the relationship between land reform and productivity will proceed in four steps: a review of the theoretical explanation of how the rent reduction will lead to an increase of land productivity (Section 1); attempts to check the change of inputs and output of the agricultural sector (Section 2) and of major crops (Section 3); and an examination of the productivity of holdings of various sizes (Section 4).

A REVIEW OF THEORY [3]

Rent reduction may take various forms. In the example worked out in Chapter 4, there are essentially two types, namely, the reduction of rate and the fixing of the base year upon which the rate is to be applied. The rent reform in Taiwan is a combination of both forms, a rent reduction from 50 per cent to 37.5 per cent to be calculated on the base-year productivity of 1948. If the productivity of land remains constant, the only benefit the tenants can realize would be from a percentage reduction of rent. However, if the land productivity increases following the land reform, as in Taiwan, the burden of rent to the tenants decreases proportionally, since the rent is a fixed charge. The distinction of these two types of rent limitation is analogous to that of a proportional income tax and a poll tax. Thus, a fixed rent has an incentive effect which can be demonstrated. [4]

It will be remembered that the above theoretical argument is a static one, whereas agriculture in Taiwan was undergoing a period of rapid change following the land reform. It is difficult, if not impossible, to disentangle the static effects from the dynamic changes. Those same reform measures that give incentive to the tenants and owner-cultivators to increase the labor and capital inputs should also induce them to improve the quality of such inputs. In particular, after land reform, the farmers were more anxious to find out about the latest information on improved seeds and on the technique of insecticide application and to follow closely the instructions of arriving at the right mixture of fertilizers and applying them at the right time. Agricultural technology will have no impact on the output until it is received and practiced by the farmers on a large scale, and the job of dissemination becomes much easier if the farmers are ready and eager to have it. There can be no doubt that part of the increase of output in Taiwan should be directly traced to technological progress (broadly defined), but the extent of its impact would certainly be different had there been no incentive effect from land reform. To the extent that static and dynamic influences are intertwined, we shall review efforts to decompose the agricultural output increase into components attributable to land, labor, capital, and technological change in the period after the land reform. Such increases will be put in historical perspective in view of the importance of the role of dynamic change.

CHANGE OF AGGREGATE INPUTS AND OUTPUTS

The indexes of farm inputs and output are available for the period 1953–60 and are shown in Table 17. The rent reduction was initiated in 1949. The use of 1953 as the base period tends to make one underestimate the increase because some increases must have taken place from 1949 to 1953. Nevertheless, labor and capital inputs do show substantial increases, while land input, as anticipated, remains unchanged. The increase of labor input was approximately 10 per cent in the seven-year span. If chemical fertilizers, seeds, animal feeds, and materials are considered a part of the capital input, the increase was especially significant in materials and fertilizers. In 1958 and 1959, it was a 40 per cent increase (Column 3). In over-all input, the increase was about 11 per cent.

Upon closer examination of the labor input data, the increase in labor input involves both an increase in the number of farm workers (from 1,427,000 workers in 1953 to 1,486,000 in 1960) and an increase in the number of workdays on the farm.[5] Moreover, the increase in the workdays is larger than that of the number of workers. Consequently, we find that the number of workdays (on the farm) per worker per year was 173 in 1953 and 181 in 1960. These figures mean that not only were there more farmworkers in 1960 than in 1953 but also each worked a little harder (about eight more days a year on the average).

On the basis of the aggregate data of the agricultural sector, we have witnessed some increases in both inputs (by 11 per cent from 1953 to 1960) and output (by 23 per cent for the same period), and the increase of outputs is greater than that of input (Column 12), a fact not at variance with what we

Table 17

Comparison of Indexes of Farm Inputs and Output,* 1953-60

(1953 = 100)

Year	(1) Land Input	(2) Labor Input	(3) Chemical Fertilizer	(4) Seed	(5) Animal Feed	(6) Cattle Input	(7) Deprec- iation Equipment	(8) Mater- ials	(9) Irrigation Drainage	(10) Total Input	(11) Total Output	(12) (11)/(10) x 100
1953	100	100	100	100	100	100	100	100	100	100	100	100
1954	100	100	118	101	104	106	98	165	99	101	100	99
1955	100	98	120	99	106	106	96	254	98	103	99	96
1956	100	102	131	101	112	106	97	224	100	106	108	102
1957	100	109	135	106	120	106	98	279	101	109	115	106
1958	101	112	140	107	131	107	101	376	101	113	122	108
1959	101	111	139	107	126	108	94	390	100	112	122	109
1960	100	109	124	110	126	108	92	504	105	111	123	111

* Indexes of inputs and index of total output are based on estimates by the Rural Economics Division of JCRR. In Column 12, total output is divided by total input and then multiplied by 100.

Source: *Economic Bulletin for Asia and The Far East*, XIV, No. 1 (June, 1963), p. 60.

expected. If such an index is extended to cover the period of 1901-60 (with the base year shifted to 1903 = 100), one notes that most, if not all, of the achievement took place in the two periods of 1926-40 and 1951-60.[6] The 1926-40 period can easily be identified with the irrigation development in the 1920's and 1930's;[7] the impetus given to the agriculture in the 1950's by the land reform, therefore, cannot be ruled out as the prime cause.

One attempt to go beyond the aggregate yield and decompose the sources of the increased yield was made by Ho, but he did not approach the problem by a statistically fitted production function. Instead, he compiled an aggregate input index covering the span of 1901-60 and based on the geometric formula (1):

$$I_t = \frac{i_t}{i_o} = \frac{1^{x_t^a} \cdot 2^{x_t^b} \cdot 3^{x_t^c}}{1^{x_o^a} \cdot 2^{x_o^b} \cdot 3^{x_o^c}}$$

In the formula, $_i x_t$ stands for input i in physical unit at time t; a, b, c, ... is each an average factor share or the arithmetic mean of the cost of each factor in the total cost of production. The following result (2) was obtained:

$$I_t = 1^{x_t^{0.2462}} \cdot 2^{x_t^{0.4524}} \cdot 31^{x_t^{0.1929}} \cdot 32^{x_t^{0.1085}}$$

In this equation, $_i x_t = {_i x_t}/{_i x_o}$ and each i (i = 1, 2, 31, and 32) stands for land, labor, working and fixed capitals in physical units in year t.[9]

Since the equation is not fitted statistically, it provides no correlation coefficient or standard error of estimates for evaluating the significance of the coefficient or how well the function fits the data, but it is an extremely simple method to follow. The form of the equation has the advantage that the individual relative growth components are additive, allowing the contribution of neutral technological change (broadly defined) and the ratio of changes in each of the inputs to the changes in output to be determined. By using discrete year-to-year change as an approximation, we can work out a numerical example based on 1950-60 aggregate input-output data in Taiwan.

First, we rewrite equation 2 in the following form (3):

$$\bar{I} = 0.2462\bar{X}_1 + 0.4524\bar{X}_2 + 0.3014\bar{X}_3$$

The bars indicate the annual rates of change of I, X_1, X_2, and X_3.[10] The form is simple enough that a direct application of the relative-factor share weights to the percentage increase of each of the input categories gives us the contribution of each input to the relative expected output growth for the period under study. Second, to explain the observed input-output relationship, a constant should be inserted into equation 3 to account for the difference between the observed and the expected outputs to which we shall attribute technological change (broadly defined). Thus, we have equation 4:

$$q_t = q_t' + I_t q_o$$

Here, q_t equals the observed output at year t, $I_t q_o$ equals the expected output based on the inputs index, assuming no technological change, and q_t' equals the unexplained output which is considered the result of technological change. Expressing equation 4 in relative terms, we have equation 5:[11]

$$\frac{q_t}{q_o} = \frac{q_t'}{q_o} + I_t \text{ or } \bar{Q}_t = \bar{Q}_t' + \bar{I}_t$$

Using the input indexes for land and labor (Table 18) and the capital index derived therefrom,[12] we arrive at the figures in Table 18. The average output for 1956-60 relative to 1953 is higher by 18 per cent, of which 4 per cent was due to the increase of labor, 10 per cent to the increase of capital, and the remaining 4 per cent to broadly defined technological changes and assumed to be neutral. Thus, roughly one half of the increase came from capital increase, and labor increase and technological change were each one quarter of the output growth. The picture does not seem unreasonable for the agricultural sector as a whole because rice, the main crop in Taiwan, was the most capital intensive of all crops and accounts for most of the increased productivity of the agricultural sector.

Table 18
Components of Output Growth, 1956-60

| Year | Output Growth (1953=100) | Contribution (by per cent) | | | Techno-logical Change |
		Land (5/20)	Labor (9/20)	Capital (6/20)	
1956	108	0	0.9	6.9	0.2
1957	115	0	4.1	8.1	2.8
1958	122	0.3	5.4	11.7	5.0
1959	122	0.3	5.0	10.5	6.2
1960	123	0	4.1	10.8	8.1
Average	118	0.1	3.9	9.8	4.4
	100	1	21	54	24

Source: Table 16.

As a means to further assess the dynamic impact of land reform on yield, we shall compare, through various periods in Taiwan, the rate of technological change (broadly defined); i.e., the part of observed output unexplained by the conventional input.[13] The rates of technical progress (compounded) for these periods are: 1901-60, 1.1 per cent; 1946-60, 3.2 per cent; and 1951-60, 2.7 per cent.[14] It is reasonable to assume that, historically, the rate of technological changes is much below that of 1946-60, because 1946, an immediate post-World War II year, had a low output base. Much of the growth can be attributed to rehabilitation and recovery. However, the rate of 2.7 per cent in 1951-60, although lower than that of 1946-60, is 1.6 per cent higher than the historical trend.

We made some reservation earlier regarding the reliability of the numerical coefficients in our example because of the limitation of the approach. Yet, the estimated shares are not out of line with results obtained elsewhere[15] and the rate of change of technological progress during the period of 1951-60 is sufficiently higher than that shown in the historical trend; so the possible dynamic impact of land reform on agricultural yield cannot be completely dismissed.

So far, our evidence has been confined to aggregate statistics. We must now, therefore, turn to the productivity data of the major crops in Taiwan.

INPUTS AND OUTPUTS OF MAJOR CROPS

The production data on each of the two major common and special crops, i.e., rice and sweet potatoes (common crops) and sugar cane and peanuts (special crops), will be examined. The importance of these major crops to the agricultural income should be emphasized. Take the value of agricultural income in 1961, for example. The percentage for rice was 44.33, sweet potatoes 8.66, sugar cane 6.23, and peanuts 2.94. The combined value of these crops totals 62.16 per cent of the agricultural output, or 86.82 per cent of the value of common and special crops.[16]

Since it is quite possible that the increased output of an individual crop is due to an expansion of acreage at the expense of other crops, we shall concentrate our attention on yield instead of on the total output of a crop. To even out yearly fluctuations, a series of five-year average outputs per hectare for rice, sweet potatoes, peanuts, and sugar cane since 1900 was derived. By taking the first differences, we note the change of crop productivity for each successive period. In rice, for example, the incremental change for successive five-year intervals at 244 kilograms per hectare was largest in the 1930's for the fifty-year period that the island was under the Japanese control.[17] Then, there was a sudden reduction of productivity during World War II and a further drop during the period immediately following the war. After 1949, the yield began to surge and continue to surge.

If we take the increase of productivity measured by successive five-year intervals since 1949 as the gains from land reform, i.e., 514 kilograms from 1945-49 to 1950-54, we would obviously be exaggerating the contribution of land reform since we have not fully discounted the rise from an extremely low base-period of the World War II aftermath. Even the change of 319 kilograms between the periods of 1950-54 and 1955-59 is perhaps an inflated figure, since in the late 1930's the average productivity per hectare reached the higher figure of 2,052 kilograms. A more reasonable approach is to take the highest pre-war figure of 2,052 kilograms and compare it with 2,322 kilograms to have a difference of 270 kilograms, which is higher by 26 kilograms than the highest five-year period change, 244 kilograms, reached since 1900.

Comparing the change of rice productivity on a worldwide basis, the achievement in Taiwan is an impressive one. Of the thirteen major rice-producing countries (1 million acres or more in rice) only two, namely, Japan and the United States, did better in terms of the change of the rice yield from 1935-39 to 1960-62.[18,19]

When we separate the productivity data into first and second crops and paddy and upland rice,[20] and apply the same analysis we used for the aggregate data, we find that the change of yield was by no means uniform. A much higher rate of productivity change took place in the first crop than in the second. Furthermore, all of the increase in yield occurred in the paddy fields because the productivity in the 1955-59 period for upland rice was still below the rate in the late 1920's and the 1930's. Incidentally, the average productivity of brown paddy rice per hectare in 1955-59 was 2,376 kilograms, which is 26 kilograms higher than the highest average production per hectare, 2,079 kilograms, ever reached for paddy rice in the late 1930's.

Analysis of productivity data of sweet potatoes shows that the change of productivity from 1945-49 to 1950-54 was a modest one of 670 kilograms.[21] A spectacular increase took place in the 1955-59 period over the previous one (2,511 kilograms), and it is the highest increase in the record. But the absolute yield per hectare, 11,714 kilograms per hectare, was still 229 kilograms below the peak achieved in the late 1930's. The data on peanuts[22] disclose a similar pattern. The recovery of yield per hectare was high—an increase of 152 kilograms between 1950-54 and 1955-59, although not the highest on record. As in the case of sweet potatoes, the output per hectare in 1955-59 was still below the peak of 959 kilograms in 1935-39.

The sugar cane data are more difficult to assess.[23] The rate of increase in yield in the post-World War II years was high. The average yield in 1955-59 passed the record achieved in the late 1930's by 4,812 kilograms, which was well within the rate of increase of the entire time series under observation. Another complication in evaluating the possible impact of land reform on the yield of sugar cane was the predominance of sugar-cane farms owned and operated by the Taiwan Sugar Company. The frequent introduction of new sugar-cane varieties and disappearance of the old ones may account for the increase of productivity, instead of land reform.

Insofar as sweet potatoes and peanuts were concerned, we find that we have no evidence of increase in productivity after the land reform. However, the data on brown-rice productivity, especially of paddy rice and first crop, indicated a sufficient increase in productivity after the land reform to warrant the inference of a favorable impact of land reform on rice yield.[24]

A study of the productivity data of the major crops reveals differentials between crops. Since the above data are in terms of land productivity, can this lack of uniformity in productivity increase be explained by the tenants' incentive in applying more labor and capital and in learning new agricultural practices?

Among the crops, the elasticity of output to the change of labor and capital input varies. Capital and labor will be allocated among crops to the point that a marginal unit will yield the same marginal value output. The observed pattern of increase of land productivity for the three main crops (rice, sweet potatoes, and peanuts) suggests either that the rice output was more responsive to the increase of capital and, to a lesser extent, labor, than the other crops (assuming that the relative prices remained unchanged) or that the rice field could absorb more capital and labor before the marginal value of the last unit of capital and labor inputs becomes the same as that employed in the production of sweet potatoes and peanuts.[25]

Agricultural technology supports profitability by allocating more capital and labor to rice than other crops. There is uncertainty in what a farmer can expect to get from fertilizer application to crops such as sweet potatoes and peanuts which are grown entirely on dry land with no supplementary irrigation. In years with plenty of rainfall at the right time, extra investment in fertilizers, etc., in the dry-land crops will pay off. But the returns are much more risky than those from investment in the paddy fields.

If relative capital intensity indeed explains the difference in yield between rice and the other crops, how do we account for the difference in yield between the first and the second crops of rice and between the paddy and upland rice? There is evidence of slightly lower labor input per hectare of the second crop than that of the first. The reduction is about 5 per cent.[26] The most important factor, however, is rice variety. The weather for the first rice crop in Taiwan is generally temperate and for the second rice crop, tropical. As the present Ponlai varieties are derived from a temperate-zone ancestry, new crossbreeds from the tropical regions are needed to boost the low yield of the second rice crop, which must endure all the severities of a tropical season. New rice varieties are being developed that will be adapted to the weather conditions of the second crop.[27] In the future, it will be of interest to compare two varieties under comparable environments.

As for the upland rice, it is grown on dry land and subject to the same uncertainty of getting a reasonable return on the investment in fertilizers, etc., as other dry-land crops such as sweet potatoes and peanuts, which were discussed earlier. More important as an explanation in our present context is the pattern of landownership between paddy fields and dry land before the land reform. The absentee landlords were only interested in investing in paddy fields, not in dry land. According to the statistics of the land compulsorily purchased from the landlords by the government, out of the the total 143,468 hectares, 85 per cent was paddy fields, the rest being dry land. Most of the new owners were, therefore, purchasers of paddy fields. As a result, the increased productivity of paddy fields following the land reform would be more easily noticed in the over-all yield figures than those of dry land, where the new owner-purchasers occupied a small percentage of the total of such land.

In conclusion, our findings on the output change and yield of major crops demonstrate the capital- and labor-using nature of paddy-rice production. In view of the weight of the paddy-rice output carried in the total agricultural output, the relatively large contribution of capital input to the increase of aggregate agricultural output, as shown in Section 2, is understandable. Furthermore, nothing is found in the major crop data that appears to have been at variance with the weights assigned to the contribution of labor input and technology (e.g., new rice varieties, fertilizer, and insecticide application) to the output.

FARM SIZE AND LAND PRODUCTIVITY

Concomitant with land reform was wider distribution of landownership and reduction in size of holdings, as shown in Chapter 3. In the long run, population pressure and lack of employment opportunities in the nonagricultural sectors may be more decisive factors than the land reform in land fragmentation. Of course, land reform must have accelerated the trend. Thus, the study of farm size and land productivity takes on added

significance as a basic economic problem of the densely populated underdeveloped countries. Surprisingly, the evidence on
yields on a per chia basis during four recent years indicates
that the landholdings of sizes below 0.49 chia enjoyed the
highest productivity per unit of land for both the first and
second rice crops. The productivity declined, with few exceptions, as the size of holdings increased. Figure 2 is a graphic
representation of the data.[28]

The result should be interpreted with care[29] and should not
be used to minimize the general unfavorable consequences on
productivity that fragmentation will entail. Remember that the
immediate rise of small holdings in Taiwan is the result of the
sale of public land and the land-to-the-tiller program. The new
owners are generally small landholders, and most of the land
held formerly by absentee landlords and sold was of two crops.
In fact, a higher per cent of land on the small farm is of two
or more crops than on the large farm.[30] In a sample study of
1,144 farms in Taiwan classified according to size, it was found
that in the size interval under 0.499 chia, 63 per cent of the
land was of two or more crops and that the per cent went down
as the holding size interval increased until the per cent of two-
crop land reached 17 per cent for holdings of more than 7
chias.[31]

Another explanation is that perhaps the incentive effect
of being owner-cultivators for the first time (largely small ones)
made them all the more willing to increase capital and labor inputs and to find out about seeds and fertilizer utilization in
increasing the yield of the farm.[32] Of course, we can argue as
Johnson did[33] that owners of small holdings have to work harder
in order to achieve a minimum standard of living. The assertion
implies that the preference map between work and income may
change as a person's holdings vary.[34] In fact, empirical evidence bears out the contention that the smaller the size of the
farm, the more labor was used on a per hectare basis, as shown
in Table 19. However, the figures in the second column,
strictly speaking, are not comparable because small holdings
consist of a higher per cent of multiple-crop land than large
holdings. But even after adjusting labor input on a per crop
hectare basis, we still find that the average units of labor input
per crop hectare are larger for small than for large holdings.
In the farm survey referred to earlier, further refinements of
labor requirements of landholdings into double- and single-crop
land, dry land, and orchards showed a similar picture of more
labor input per chia for small than for large holdings.[35]

FIGURE 2
SIZE OF HOLDINGS AND YIELD OF PADDY RICE, 1958–62

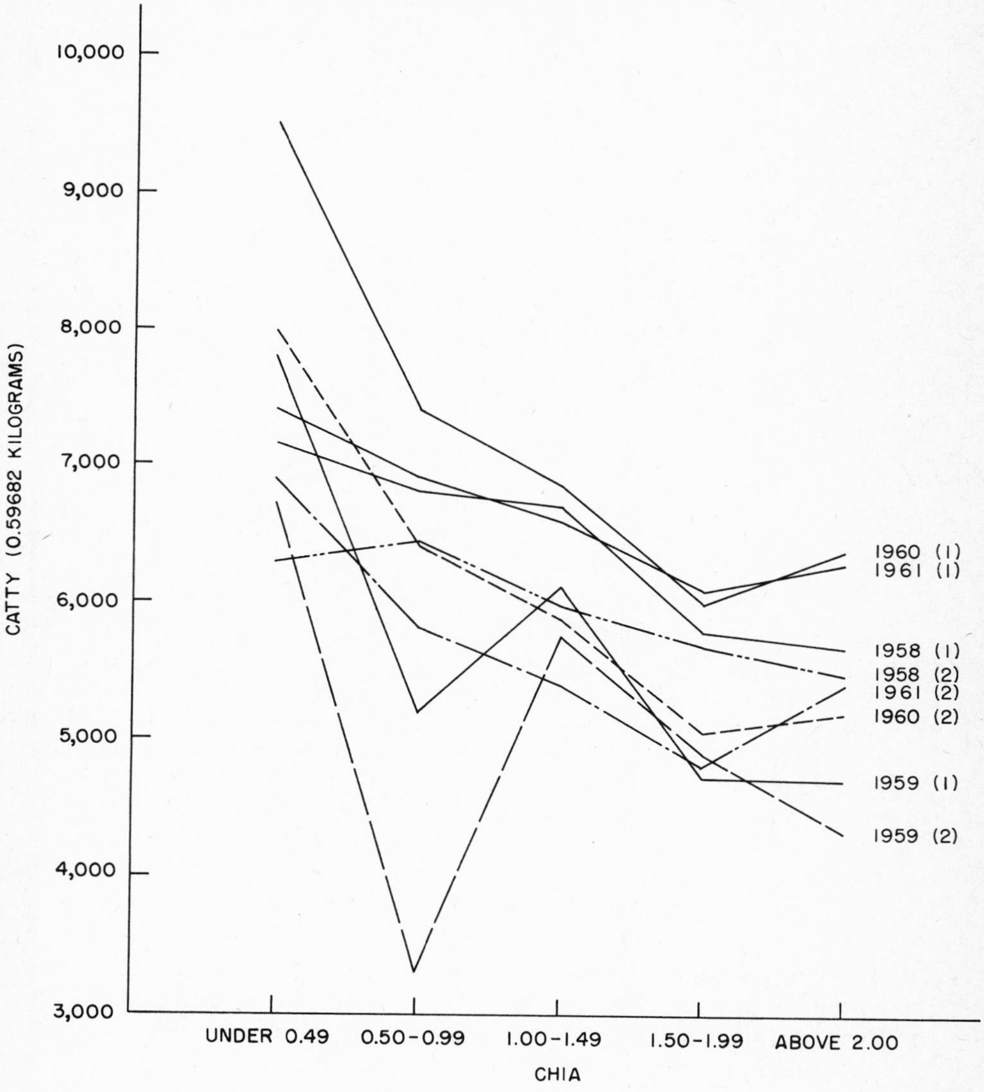

Table 19
Size of Holdings and Labor Inputs

Size of Holdings (chia)	Average Units of Labor* per Hectare	Average Units of Labor per Crop Hectare
Below 0.51	893	387
0.52–1.03	613	256
1.04–1.54	412	179
1.55–2.06	331	150
2.07 and above	313	146
Average (weighted)	387	176

* A unit of labor is defined as ten hours of work for a male worker. A female worker's hours are converted to the unit of labor at an 80 per cent ratio.

Source: *Agriculture Census 1961*, Taipei, Taiwan.

A warning should be made against possible misinterpretation that might be read into the data. The table does not show that the labor input of each farm family on small holdings is larger than that of large holdings. Because of the variation in farm size, it takes more families of small landholdings to take up a given area than those of large holdings. Thus, when labor utilization is put on a per family basis, each family of small holdings utilizes a smaller amount of its available labor supply because of the physical restriction imposed by the holding size than a family of larger holdings (within certain range). The implications of farm size and rural unemployment will be discussed in Chapter 7.

SUMMARY AND CONCLUSION

The present chapter reviewed some theoretical arguments by which we tested the impact of land reform on productivity. We started with the aggregate data of input and output for the agricultural sector as a whole and proceeded to the productivity of the main crops. The findings indicate a general increase of agricultural productivity in the past decade, with the increase of capital input being a more important element than either the increase of labor input or technological progress. Of all crops, rice productivity has risen more than ever before since land reform. We do not contend that land reform is the sole contributory factor in this achievement. Rather, it is significantly correlated with such other factors as improved rice varieties, dissemination of technology in the use of fertilizers and insecticides, etc., which can cause quick increase of the agricultural output, in general, and the productivity of the first crop paddy rice, in particular.

The argument that a division of farm land into smaller units would cause a decline in productivity is based on the assumption that there are economies of large-scale production. The assumption is generally valid in industrialized countries such as the United States and has been put forth occasionally as an argument against land reform on the grounds of possible loss of land productivity. The data in Taiwan do not support this contention. The finding, however, should not be interpreted as a denial of the importance of scale of the agricultural unit. It simply means that the optimum scale of agricultural output is difficult to define precisely because of the diversified conditions in many lands. Nor is there evidence in Taiwan that tenants took advantage of rent reduction to enjoy more leisure. On the contrary, they seemed to have put in more capital and labor per unit of land and to have been anxious to learn modern agricultural practices. Such behavior is largely due to the incentive effect of fixed rent coupled with the reduction of the average holdings per family under the land-to-the-tiller program.

CHAPTER 6 FINANCING DEVELOPMENT

Taiwan has built many multiple purpose reservoirs designed to serve a combined purpose of irrigation, industrial water supply, flood control, and power generation. They are often pointed to as excellent examples of the contribution of agriculture to the growth of the nonagricultural sectors in the development process. It is argued that without the multiple use of water for power generation and irrigation, some of the projects could not have been economically justified. Conspicuous as these examples are, a more important contribution of agriculture occurs when it transfers capital to other parts of the economy.

In the present chapter, we shall discuss the contribution of agriculture after the land reform to financing economic development under the headings: (1) farmland as a medium of private investment, (2) compulsory transfers from agriculture to the other sectors, (3) the flow of savings between the sectors, and (4) supply of total savings.

FARMLAND AS A MEDIUM OF PRIVATE INVESTMENT

Before the land reform, the record in Taiwan shows that investment in farms was safe and profitable. This is perhaps true in most of the underdeveloped countries. The first source of profit arises out of appreciation of the land value. The price of a paddy field in terms of kilograms of paddy rice was 13,565 kilograms per hectare in 1914-19 (Table 20). It moved steadily upward with few exceptions and reached 20,791 kilograms of paddy rice in 1938-43—a rise of more than 50 per cent in a span of thirty years. This can be clearly shown if we express the 1914-19 price as 100. The index went to 153.27 in 1938-43. Next came the rise of the land rent, on the average of 1,821 kilograms in 1914-19 with a rise to 2,403 kilograms (an increase of 32 per cent) in 1938-43. The increase of rent was slightly below that of output by 7.5 per cent. This is all the gain for the tenants for the thirty-year period of 1914-43. Since the price of rice rose relative to other price indexes (113.1 in 1914-19 to 129.4 for the same period, or a little over 14 per cent), it represents another source of gain for the landlords.

Table 20
Price, Rent, and Output of Paddy Farms, 1914-43

Year	Price of Paddy Farm		Rent of Paddy		Output of Paddy		Price of Rice	
	kg/ha.	Index	kg/ha.	Index	kg/ha.	Index	Relative to Gen. Prices	Index
1914-17	13,565	100	1821	100	3652	100	113	100
1917-22	14,471	107	1980	109	3749	103	114	101
1920-23	13,769	102	2024	111	3927	108	111	98
1923-28	15,397	114	2051	113	4176	114	119	106
1926-31	18,810	139	2174	129	4331	119	112	99
1929-34	20,142	148	2387	131	4649	127	109	96
1932-37	20,049	148	2590	142	5041	138	134	119
1935-40	22,387	165	2623	144	5241	144	144	127
1938-43	20,791	153	2403	132	5096	140	129	114

Source: T. H. Lee and Y. T. Chen, "Structure of Income Distribution in Taiwan Agricultural Sector" (in Chinese), *Cooperative Quarterly*, 26, pp. 4-5.

Land reform immediately changed the picture. The program of limiting rent to 37.5 per cent of the average yield for 1948 made land investment closer to the nature of fixed-income bonds rather than common stocks because any increase in the productivity of land, unless reassessed and certified by the public authorities, goes to the tenants rather than the landlords. So far in Taiwan, the 1948 yield is still the basis for rent calculation. The implication of land reform on financing economic development is that rent limitation lowers the opportunity cost of investment in the nonagricultural sector, thus encouraging an increase in investment in such areas.

COMPULSORY TRANSFERS FROM AGRICULTURE

An estimate of the income and savings of the agricultural sector for selected years was shown in Table 16. Here we shall attempt to trace the flow of the agricultural surplus, including the transfer of savings from the agricultural sector to the nonagricultural. The transfer can take on many forms, such as the terms of trade between the agricultural and nonagricultural products, in general, and the barter ratio between rice and fertilizer, in particular; and the relative tax burden between the two sectors of economy, in general, and the prices of those portions of rice subject to compulsory purchase by the government, in specific. Thus, our evaluation of the contribution of the agricultural sector to the financing of development in the other parts of the economy is incomplete without some reference to the contribution in the above-mentioned forms.

We have no data on the relative price ratio between the agricultural goods and nonagricultural goods to show the terms of trade between the two. What we can get is the relative price between the agricultural products and all commodities. A summary by decades is shown in Table 21 and by the yearly fluctuations in Appendix 8. It is interesting to note that except for a brief flurry of price rise in a few years, the price that the farmer in Taiwan has received has been below the base period of 1935-37. For most years, the prices were in the range of eighties and nineties of the index points. In the period following the land reform, the relative price of agricultural products fell even further (66.05) than ever before. The fact suggests that the agricultural sector's contribution to the nonagricultural sector is more than that indicated by the amount of transfers estimated in the following sections of the present chapter.

Table 21
Relative Price Index of Agricultural
Products in Terms of All Commodities, 1911-60
(1935-37 = 100)

Year	Relative Index
1911–20	91.87
1921–30	94.71
1931–40	93.64
1941–50	80.30
1951–60	66.05

Source: Appendix Table 8.

We shall begin with an estimate of compulsory transfers by using the data on the barter ratio between paddy rice and commercial fertilizer. The farmers in Taiwan get commercial fertilizers from the government agencies in exchange for rice. The system was initiated in 1948 and administered by the Taiwan Sugar Corporation with the sugar-cane growers. The barter ratio is set by the government agencies each year in accordance with the type of the chemical fertilizer.[1]

In order to determine the extent to which the barter ratio deviates from one that expresses the relative market price, four sets of estimates were made for ten chemicals, based on the figure of 1960.[2] We find that the existing barter price for fertilizer is higher in terms of rice than the ratio based on the market prices of rice and fertilizers, except in the case of fused phosphate, which is the same. Take the 1959 barter ratio, for example. The differences expressed in percentage terms range from 11.2 above the market price for calcium super phosphate to 33.3 above for ammonium sulphate. Using the fertilizer consumption pattern of 1959, we estimate the rice collected under the existing barter ratio and compare it with that collected under the market ratio. The excess of the rice collected under the former ratio over that of the latter is 101,000 metric tons of rice.[3] At the price of NT$1,000 per metric ton, we arrive at a total value of about NT$404 million in one year's compulsory transfer from the barter between rice and fertilizer.

Before summarizing such transfers for the 1950's, we turn to other sources and forms of compulsory transfer so that stock can be taken at the end of all compulsory transfers and some economic implications evaluated. The tax burden of the agricultural and the industrial sectors can only be determined approximately, if at all. A crude approximation is obtained from the per cent of government revenue derived directly from each sector. For example, we consider land tax to fall primarily on the agricultural sector and the business tax on the industrial sector. In 1950, 9.4 per cent of the total revenue of the government was derived from the land tax and 3.4 per cent from business. It was 6.2 per cent for the former and 4.5 per cent for the latter in 1960. But it is unsatisfactory to use such measures as an indication of the relative burdens for two main reasons. First, both taxes combined constitute only a little over 10 per cent of the total government revenue. The relative burdens of some of the more sizable taxes, such as custom duties (15.8 per cent), commodity tax (12.1 per cent), defense surtax (10.8 per cent), etc., are difficult to ascertain.[4] Secondly, the other side of the general tax burden is the benefit of government expenditure which should be matched against the relative burdens. Its allocation in terms of the relative benefit to the agricultural and to the nonagricultural sectors is far from simple.

However, as a more specific illustration, we consider the price received by the farmers on the portion of rice compulsorily purchased by the government and paid to the government as land tax, rent on public land, and land cost repayment. The sum is not insignificant, for more than 80 per cent of the farmers in Taiwan are rice farmers. The price they receive from the government has been about 30 per cent below the market price. The spread varied from year to year, as shown in Column 7, Table 22. To express it in value terms, we multiply the price spread by the number of tons of rice collected under different headings, the sum of which is shown in Column 6. The total value for each year of 1951-60 is listed in Column 8. Table 23 adds the surplus transferred under both the barter between rice and fertilizer and the rice compulsorily purchased and collected as taxes or rent. The details of the procedure for calculating the differentials between the market and barter prices for fertilizers will not be followed for all years of 1951-60. Instead, we estimate the number of tons of rice received under fertilizer barter by the government and multiply each yearly figure by the price differentials we used in estimating the gains to the government under the compulsory purchase and tax collection.[5] The value of total compulsory transfer for each year since 1951 was arrived at in Column 5 of Table 23. It ranges from NT$96 million in 1951 to NT$1,283 million in 1960.

The estimates we made for the forced transfers will be combined in the next section with the flow of saving from the agricultural sector to arrive at the total transfers from agricultural to the nonagricultural sector.

FLOW OF SAVINGS BETWEEN
THE AGRICULTURAL AND NONAGRICULTURAL SECTORS

Since a direct estimate on the contribution of the savings of the agricultural sector is not feasible, we shall use an in-

Table 22
Price Differentials of Rice Collected and
Compulsorily Purchased in 1951-60

Year	(1) Land Tax	(2) Com- pulsory Pur- chase	(3) Rent on Public Land	(4) Land Cost Repay- ment	(5) Land Bond in Kind	(6) Sum (1)+(2)+ (3)+(4) −(5)	(7) Price Spread (NT$)	(8) Total Value (6)x(7) (NT$1,000)
1951	92	78	20	...	...	190	224	42,560
1952	91	78	12	...	...	181	679	122,899
1953	91	77	9	134	84	227	1,224	277,848
1954	90	76	9	121	90	206	565	116,390
1955	82	70	9	112	97	176	639	112,464
1956	89	74	10	143	98	218	813	177,234
1957	93	77	10	143	98	225	935	210,375
1958	90	75	13	133	98	213	898	191,174
1959	81	68	9	123	99	182	933	169,806
1960	83	69	9	120	98	183	2,087	381,921

Source: *Taiwan Food Statistics Book* (Taipei, 1961). For price
spread, see E. L. Rada and T. H. Lee, *Irrigation Investment in Taiwan* (Taipei: JCRR, 1963), p. 30.

direct method of estimation suggested by Kuznets. The key
elements of Kuznets' formulation for such an approximation
are three: share of agricultural product to total product,
ratio of agriculture savings to total savings, and the relative
growth rate (r) of both the agricultural and nonagricultural
sectors. He bases his method[6] on the assumption that:

The flow of savings out of the A-sector to finance
capital formation elsewhere would depend largely upon
the relative needs of these sectors for capital, as
reflected in differential rates of return (all other
conditions being abstracted from). Perhaps the incremental capital-output ratios might suggest how much
capital is needed to secure additional output. ... If
this situation can be assumed. .. , the allocation of
savings depends largely upon the relative rates of
growth of the A (agricultural) and non-A sectors,
reflecting differences in long-term demand for ad-
ditions to their product.[7]

In Taiwan, the growth rate of national income is about
8 per cent per year according to the official statistics[8] and

Table 23

Compulsory Transfers from the Agricultural to the
Nonagricultural Sectors in 1951-60

	(1)	(2)	(3)	(4)	(5)
	Rice Collected (1,000 metric tons)		Sum (1)+(2)	Price Spread (NT$)	Total Value (NT$1,000)
Year	Compulsory Purchase	Fertilizer Barter			
1951	190	239	429	224	96,096
1952	181	309	490	679	332,710
1953	227	323	550	1224	676,200
1954	206	393	559	565	338,435
1955	176	377	553	639	353,367
1956	218	418	636	813	517,068
1957	225	420	645	935	603,075
1958	213	428	641	898	575,618
1959	182	426	608	933	567,264
1960	183	432	615	2087	1283,505

Source: C. S. Shih, L. Lin, and L. H. Kou, "An Appraisal of
the Fertilizer-Rice Barter System In Taiwan,"
Journal of Social Science (in Chinese) (June, 1961), and
Table 22.

7 to 7.5 per cent if adjustment was made for underestimation of
income in the early 1950's. For the present purpose the
outcome is independent of the over-all growth rate. We shall
nevertheless use 7 per cent as an illustration. The net savings
ratio is 13.6 per cent during 1951-60.[9] This savings ratio taken
in conjunction with the national income growth rate implies
an incremental capital output ratio of 1.9 (13.6/7). On the basis
of the average of 1951-60, the rate of growth of the product of
the nonagricultural sector is seven tenths that of the product of
the agricultural sector.[10] Thus, we can calculate the needed capital formation in the agricultural sector from the equation (1):

$$sr + (1-s)\ 7/10\ r = 7.0$$

The share of the agricultural sector in income is s and r, the
rate of calculated growth of the agricultural sector. We know
that s = 0.36.[11] Substitute this s value in (1), and we have
equation (2):

$$(0.36)\ r + (0.64)\ 7/10\ r = 7.0$$

Here, r = 8.7 per cent and that for the nonagricultural seven tenths of 8.7, or 6.1 per cent. Multiplying 6.1 by 0.64 yields 3.90, the increment of the product of the nonagricultural sector. Similarly, multiplying 8.7 by 0.36 yields 3.13, the increment of the product of the agricultural sector. Accordingly, from Kuznets' assumption, the ratio of the increment in the agricultural sector to the increment in the total product divided by the ratio of the capital needs of the agricultural sector to total capital needs is then 3.13/7 = 0.45, or 45 per cent. Similarly, that of the nonagricultural sector is 3.9/7 = 0.55, or 55 per cent; whereas, the amount of savings originating in agriculture was nowhere close to 45 per cent until very recently.

We have the amount of savings of the agricultural sector for the years of 1951, 1955, and 1960. They are shown in Column 2 of Table 24 and as per cent of total savings in Column 5. The percentage increases from about 20 in 1950 to 42 in 1960, with an average rate of 28 per cent for the decade. However, we need to account for the forced transfer of savings through the price differentials for rice. We recalculate the percentage after such adjustments in Column 6 of Table 24. They range from 26 per cent in 1950 to 59 per cent in 1960, with an average rate of 40 per cent. On the basis of our estimates, we infer that there was a flow of voluntary savings, originating from the nonagricultural sector, into capital formation in the agricultural sector during the 1950's. When the flow of involuntary transfer of savings was taken into account, the trend seemed to reverse itself in the late 1950's. Taking the average figure of about 40 per cent for the decade, there was, therefore, a flow of savings from the nonagricultural sector into the agricultural sector accounting for 5 per cent of 45 per cent, or slightly over 11 per cent.

It may be argued that the government, through such agencies as the Land Bank, the Taiwan Provincial Food Bureau, the Taiwan Sugar Corporation, and the Taiwan Tobacco and Wine Monopoly Bureau, made production loans to the farmers in addition to those granted by JCRR through the farmers' association. In mentioning such agricultural credit, one is concerned not so much with the contribution the government made to the farm operation by providing the necessary funds for improvement in cultural practice, processing, and marketing [12] as with its role in offsetting its compulsory transfer from the agricultural sector to the government. In fact, whether by coincidence or design, the total government loans nearly equaled

Table 24
Percentage of Savings from the Agriculture Sector
to Total, 1951, 1955, and 1960
(Unit: millions of NT$)

Year	(1) Total Savings	(2) Savings from Agriculture	(3) Forced Transfers	(4) Adjusted Savings from Agricultural Sector (2)+(3)	(5) (2) as Per centage of (1)	(6) (4) as Per centage of (1)
1951	1,482	292*	96	388	19.70	26.18
1955	3,238	748	353	1,101	23.10	34.00
1960	7,544	3,145	1,284	4,429	41.69	58.71
Average					28.16	39.63

* 1950 figure.

Source: (1) See Footnote 8.
   (2) Same as Table 16, converted back into current New Taiwan dollars.
   (3) From Table 23.

the forced transfers.[13] But most of such loans were extended for a short duration, as they were generally repaid within a crop year. Unless there is substantial difference between the loan extended and the amount of repayment within the year, our estimate, which ignores both the loan and its repayment, suffers little inaccuracy.

The analysis so far has made no explicit mention of the capital formation financed by U.S. aid, which accounted for one quarter of the gross capital formation in Taiwan and can be regarded as an additional source of supply of savings.[14] In order to show whether our conclusion that savings originating in the nonagricultural sector flow into the agricultural sector to finance the growth of products should be qualified, we look at the distribution of U.S. aid in capital formation between the agricultural and nonagricultural sectors. Specifically, is it roughly in proportion to the respective demand for domestic savings, i.e., 45 per cent for the former and 55 per cent for the latter or is it heavily in favor of one or the other sector? If more than 45 per cent of the U.S. aid used to finance capital formation goes to the agricultural sector, this could mean that the portion of demand for savings in excess of its own supply may have been financed by the U.S. aid. Naturally, we would have strong reservations in accepting the conclusion concerning the flow of savings from the nonagricultural to the agricultural sector which was reached earlier, when no reference was made to the U.S. aid. We find that the distribution of U.S. aid for financing capital formation in the agricultural sector was never in excess of 22 per cent; the average for 1952-60 was 14.53 per cent.[15] The remaining portion of the funds was directed to the nonagricultural sector, which accounted for 85 per cent of the total. The data on the role of U.S. aid to capital formation do not seem to call for modification of our earlier finding that there was a flow of savings from the nonagricultural to the agricultural sector in the 1950's in Taiwan.

The above conclusion on the pattern of flow of savings seems to be consistent with our result in Chapter 4. It may be recalled that the increase in rice yield played a more dominant role in raising farm income during the early than the late 1950's. Rice cultivation, being capital intense, may have drawn savings to the agricultural sector, but the need for capital from outside sources must have been dampened when farm income from nonfarm sources during 1955-60 more than doubled that of 1950-55.

SUPPLY OF TOTAL SAVINGS [16]

The pattern of the flow of savings may have been reversed in the 1960's although it would have to be confirmed by further observations. For either sector, insufficiency of investable funds relative to demand will remain for some time. It is as much a question of allocation as one of over-all supply of savings, which have been handicapped for the period under study by a policy of pegging the interest rate on loans and deposits of the financial institutions far below the competitive level.[17] The bank rate on time and savings deposits is on the average (1950-62) 38 per cent of the market (Table 25). The arbitrary rate implies a partial suspension of the economic function of an interest rate as a criterion for the allocation of available investable funds to competing uses. The great disparity between the market rate and the controlled rates on bank loans indicates that the available funds are not allocated to different uses by a uniform competitive criterion. That is to say, projects which succeeded in their bid for the use of funds must have passed a competitive test that will give promise to yield a net return on investment at least equal to the market rate of interest, and the market rate is so determined that the

Table 25
Changes in Interest Rate and Time Deposit, 1949–62

Year	(1)* Time Deposit (in NT$ 1000)	(2) Increase in Time Deposit (in NT$ 1000)	(3)** Monthly Rate on Three-Month Preferential-Rate, Time Deposit (unless Otherwise Specified)	(4) Monthly Rate Charged by Private Primary Lender on Secured Loans	(5) (3)/(4)
1949					
1950	28,228	21,316	5.60	13.3	0.421
1951	173,654	145,540	4.20	9.2	0.456
1952	473,480	299,826	3.46	6.2	0.558
1953	605,421	131,941	1.83	4.5	0.406
1954	774,748	169,327	1.20	3.4	0.353
1955	875,215	100,467	1.10	3.2	0.344
1956	854,320	(–)20,895	1.00	3.3	0.300
1957	1,170,708	316,388	0.93	2.9	0.320
1958	2,113,955	943,247	1.15	3.1	0.371
1959	2,694,570	580,617	1.05	2.9	0.362
1960	3,751,824	1,057,363	1.05	3.3	0.318
1961	6,397,824	2,645,889	0.98	2.7	0.363
1962	7,893,592	1,495,768	0.86	2.4	0.358

* Including ordinary time deposits, preferential interest rate time deposits, savings deposits, and lottery time deposits. Deposits at the post offices, however, are not included.

** In 1958 and after, the interest rates are those charged by all banks other than the Bank of Taiwan for six-month time deposits because of their share in the total deposit.

Source: *Taiwan Financial Statistics Monthly* (Bank of Taiwan, various issues).

demand for capital which can pass the interest test will be exactly equal to the available supply.

An equally serious consequence of the arbitrary low interest rate is the loss of financial and banking institutions of their primary function as the collector of the savings of the community and as the lender to the investor. If we examine the increase in time deposit in Column 2 and the bank rate as percentage of the market rate, Column 5, Table 25, we find a rather close parallel between the two, i.e., a higher bank rate relative to the market rate is associated with a higher figure in increase in time deposits.[18]

It is true that the modern banking system can create credit on its own, regardless of the inflow of savings in the banking system. But if inflation is to be avoided, it can only increase the total loans, investments, and other assets by the net current savings flowing into the banking system plus some expansion in money supply to meet the increase in demand for cash balances due to the increase in real national income. Moreover, by making loan contracts effected at rates of interest which are higher than the arbitrary ceiling fixed by decree and which are legally invalid and unenforceable in the courts, the risk of the lender in the underground market is thus greatly increased. The reduced willingness to lend plus the increase in the demands for loans generated by those turned away by the banking system (because of the limited capacity to lend) would force the interest rate on the underground money market even higher than what the free competitive level would have been.

It is often claimed that the aggregate savings may be determined by the level of national income and that they are insensitive to the rate of interest. However, in Taiwan, as in most underdeveloped countries, a part of the current savings of the public is lost to investment through the hoarding of U.S. dollars brought in by the U.S. and other foreign residents. Under the combined effect of the unattractiveness of the interest rates on savings offered by the banking system and the excessively high risk of lending in the free money markets, U.S. dollars provide a better store of value than other instruments of savings offered in Taiwan. This part of savings is wasted in financing the consumption expenditure of the foreign residents and tourists in Taiwan, which otherwise would be financed by an equal amount of import surplus that would take the place of the domestic goods and services consumed by foreigners and leave the same amount of real resources available for investment purposes.[19]

Thus, even if the total amount of savings is absolutely inelastic to the interest rate, the supply of investable funds can be enlarged by directing savings away from the hoarding of U.S. notes into the domestic loan market by making the terms of holdings on the domestic currency more attractive in the form of a higher rate of returns. Furthermore, the unattractiveness of the yields on deposits and securities relative to the risks attached would divert potential savings to unproductive uses such as the construction of private residence, excessive purchase of durable consumption goods, and even hoarding of goods.

SUMMARY AND CONCLUSION

Direct contribution of agriculture to financing the growth of products of the nonagricultural sector was nil, if not negative, immediately following the land reform. Indirect contribution of land reform to promoting investment in other sectors takes the form of reducing the opportunity cost. The net flow of surplus from the agricultural to the nonagricultural sector did not come about until in the late 1950's and early 1960's. The sudden surge of demand for capital in agriculture relative to its supply may be attributable to the incentive on the part of tenants and owner-cultivators to increase investment in their farms, and that brought about a rise of farm productivity, as discussed earlier. This conclusion is not inconsistent with the findings in Chapter 4 on the change of farm income for the 1950's.

The agricultural output and surplus could have been greater had it not been for the pegged interest rate, in general, and for the existence of price differentials in rice and fertilizer, in particular. The difference between the official and market prices for rice amounts to a proportional tax to rice producers, and, as we have analyzed in Chapter 5, it has a dampening effect on output. The higher fertilizer price has the effect of making the farmers use less of it with a consequent reduction of the agricultural output. According to one estimate,[20] the price elasticity of fertilizers is greater than unity (1.4). The loss of output due to the higher barter ratio may not be inconsequential. It is easy, of course, to suggest that the price differentials be reduced or eliminated altogether, but the vital thing is to find the alternative sources of revenue in their place. This is a challenge too ambitious to be tackled here.

CHAPTER 7 UNEMPLOYMENT IN AGRICULTURE

Much has been written on the unemployment and disguised unemployment of the underdeveloped countries. Economists still seem unable to agree on the seriousness of the problem even when it exists in densely populated areas which are economically dominated by agriculture.[1] Many of the contradictory statements can be "proved" by defining disguised unemployment to suit the purpose and then selecting the appropriate examples, case studies and statistics. Ambiguities in terminology and an excess of "data" that can be variously interpreted have been the raw materials of dispute over unemployment and disguised unemployment.

The present chapter is not the place to review the literature or to settle the controversy. However, the previous discussion serves as a warning to us to more carefully describe the circumstances and conditions under which a definition applies and to relate empirical observation to theoretical definition.

In principle, labor will not be employed beyond the point where its marginal value product (MVP) equals the wage rate. The marginal value product, however, explains the size of employment, but not the wage rate, which, being a price, has to be determined by a demand function, i.e., MVP of labor and a supply function of labor. If the workers are willing to work at the prevailing wage rate but remain idle, they are considered involuntarily unemployed. This situation occurs when the demand curve for labor intersects the horizontal portion of the supply curve of labor. In measuring the magnitude of unemployment on the farm, we need to know the labor units actually employed on the farm (determined by the point of intersection of the MVP curve with the supply curve) and the available labor supply (the horizontal portion of the supply curve), the size of which is determined by the wage rate or, in its absence in a rural economy, by the MVP of labor. There are those who choose not to work under the prevailing rate of reward. In determining the available supply, they should be excluded from the labor force as voluntarily unemployed.

The term "disguised unemployment" was first coined by Joan Robinson to describe the situations of workers in developed countries who accepted inferior occupations as a result of having been laid off from industries suffering from insufficient effective demand.[2] The number of laid-off workers who take less than the MVP of labor that could have been achieved measures the magnitude of disguised unemployment. Many writers have since used the term "disguised unemployment" to describe the existence of (1) the labor force which can be removed without reducing output, assuming that no other changes occur *(ceteris paribus)*, (2) a situation in which the prevailing wage rate exceeds MVP of labor.

The two usages are not incompatible with one another, but the former generally refers to family labor, while the latter pertains to hired labor on the farm. Inability or failure to measure separately MVP of family and hired labor in peak and off seasons of a year is a source of much confusion in the discussion of disguised unemployment.

The first usage clearly implies that there exists labor which is being employed in the productive process but whose marginal physical product (MPP) is zero. Consequently, attention has been directed to the investigation of conditions under which MPP could be zero. For example, it is argued that such zero MPP will be attained when the total product of the family farm is maximized, and family farms constitute the great majority in Taiwan. This practice is not uncommon in the rural area since each household is under obligation to take care of all its members.[3]

The second situation exists because of the highly seasonal nature of labor demand on the farm. In areas of intensive land utilization (double or triple cropping), as in Taiwan, one of the most important organizational problems is to ensure that labor and other resources are available at exactly the right time. As described in Chapter 3, the time available for certain crucial work is severely limited, especially at the summer period of the first harvest and second sowing. Dislocation of work at any

one peak season will affect the entire agricultural output for
the year. On many farms, outside labor has to be hired at
the peak season. Thus, when one assumes the existing agricultural practice and crops as given and counts the contribution of hired labor at the peak season of farm activity, it is
doubtful that the prevailing wage rate substantially exceeds
the MVP of hired labor. It is mostly during the nonpeak season that the prevailing wage rate tends to exceed hired labor's
contribution. In Taiwan, it is uncommon practice for the
family farm to retain hired labor in any significant amount
during that period. Only when one uses the MVP of part-time
hired labor prorated over a twelve-month period does the
prevailing wage rate naturally appear to be in excess of the
MVP of hired labor. In fact, in a recent study, positive MVP
(accordingly positive MPP) based on production-function analysis was found to exist side by side with a chronic visible
underemployment of family labor.[4] Consequently, the author
of the study recommends neither zero MPP nor the difference
between MVP and prevailing wage rate as satisfactory tests
of the extent or seriousness of disguised unemployment in
Taiwan.[5]

In the light of the above discussion, in this chapter we
shall examine a sample survey of farm employment (labor utilization) in Taiwan, not so much for the result as to present a
numerical illustration of the immediate consequence of land
reform on agricultural unemployment. We do not claim that
the illustrative method is necessarily relevant to other
regions. Much depends upon whether the agricultural practice
and the state of labor supply are similar to those in Taiwan.
To complete the discussion on the subject, the long-run impact
of land reform on labor mobility will be explored and an estimate made of out-migration from agriculture in Taiwan.

MEASUREMENT OF FARM UNEMPLOYMENT
IN TAIWAN

According to a recent survey of farm labor requirements
in Taiwan, the key factors that influence the labor input are
size of holdings and type of land, which, in turn, determine
the crops. In Table 26, we have an estimate of available labor
supply for each farm household, classified in accordance with
the class interval of landholdings. In the sample, the size of
holdings seems to be related to the size of the family, up to

Table 26

Availability and Utilization of On-Farm and Off-Farm Labor
(An Estimate of Involuntarily Unemployed Labor in Agriculture)

(1) Farm Size (chia)	(2) Number of Sample Farm Families	(3) Total Potential Labor Units (Per Farm Family)	(4) Actual Utilization on and off Farm (Per Farm Family)	On Farm	Off Farm	(5) Percentage of Utilization [(4)/(3) x 100]	(6) Percentage of Involuntary Unemployed [76.99 per cent-(5)]	(7) Units of Involuntary Unemployed [(6)x(3) or (8)-(4)]	(8) Available Units of Labor [(3)x76.99 per cent]	(9) Percentage of Utilization [(4)/(8) x 100]
(1) -0.499	137	750.75	317.92	146.26	171.66	42.38	34.64	260.06	577.98	55.01
(2) 0.5-0.999	333	856.81	422.76	267.15	156,61	49.34	27.65	236.91	659.67	64.09
(3) 1.0-1.499	245	917.04	532.23	404.55	127.68	58.04	18.95	173.78	706.01	75.32
(4) 1.5-1.999	180	985.61	635.04	494.83	140.21	64.43	12.56	123.79	755.83	84.02
(5) 2.0-2.499	103	1168.30	754.39	589.02	165.37	64.57	12.42	145.10	899.49	83.83
(6) 2.5-2.999	63	1134.31	771.57	636.14	135.43	68.02	8.97	101.75	873.32	88.35
(7) 3.0-3.499	34	1177.31	830.96	654.32	176.64	70.58	6.41	75.47	906.45	91.67
(8) 3.5-3.999	21	1266.57	958.43	763.23	191.20	75.67	1.32	16.72	975.15	98.29
(9) 4.0-4.499	14	1110.22	854.77	805.41	49.36	76.99	0	0	854.77	100.00
(10) 4.5-6.499	10	1584.00	1029.03	837.71	141.32	64.96	....*	....*	1029.03**	100.00
(11) 6.5-	4	936.38	587.69	431.69	156.00	62.76	....*	....*	587.69**	100.00
	1,144									

* The heading does not apply to the figure.

* The figures are those in Column 4.

Source: C. K. Wu and T. K. Lee, *The Demand and Supply of Farm Labor of the Families of the Vocational Students* (in Chinese) (Taichung: Chung Hsin University, 1963).

Notes to Table 26

The sample size is 4.62 per cent of the total population (24,764 farm families of agricultural vocational students) who had been trained to keep detailed farm accounts. The labor requirements were estimated on a twelve-month basis, specifically February 1, 1961, to January 31, 1962, and covered the following categories of work: growing of crops and vegetables; care of water buffaloes, livestock, poultry, and orchards; and food processing. Adjustments were made for differences in land composition for each class interval. On the average, two-crop land was estimated to require 23 per cent more labor per chia and one-crop land, 7 per cent more labor per chia than dry land.

Labor units are calculated in accordance with the following criteria:

1. Account was taken of all male and female members of the family between the ages of twelve and sixty inclusive.

2. The hours of female members between sixteen and sixty are converted to the unit of labor at an 80 per cent ratio to males. Children (regardless of sex) between twelve and sixteen years of age are counted as equivalent to 0.50 male adult; full-time students, 0.25 and 0.50 for boarding at school or home, respectively. Those in the armed forces are completely excluded.

3. Allowance was made for the housekeeping labor requirement for each farm family as follows:

Number of People per Family	Adult Women
5 and under	0.5
6-9	1.0
10-14	1.5
15-19	2.0
20-24	2.5
25 and over	3.0

4. Each adult male is supposed to work ten hours a day and 330 days a year.

5. A detailed schedule specifying the labor requirement for each crop and farm operation is not reproduced here. The limitations of Wu-Lee's method of calculating the labor requirement are examined in the text.

* * *

and including the fifth group (2.0-2.49 chia). The survey arrived at the actual utilization figure for each class by accounting for work both on and off the farm. The percentage of labor utilization (Column 5) was calculated by expressing the figures in Column 4 as a percentage of those in Column 3. It is of interest to note that there is a pattern of rising rate of utilization from 42.35 per cent in the first group to a peak of 76.99 per cent in the ninth group, and then it tapers off to 62.76 per cent in the 6.5 chia and above groups.

Wu and Lee use the labor utilization rate of the ninth group, i.e., 76.99 per cent as the norm in their analysis. The decision is somewhat arbitrary, notwithstanding 76.99 per cent being the highest rate of labor utilization in the sample. The reason is that per cent of labor utilization is not entirely independent of wage rate, "irksomeness" of labor and the relative price between labor and capital. In fact, the decline of labor utilization rate in groups larger than the ninth might be due to the feasibility of using agricultural machinery on larger farms. Thus, one should not put much faith in the constant 76.99 per cent but should prefer a figure variable with the factors mentioned above. This reservation will certainly cast doubt on the significance of their quantitative findings but should not deter us from using their figures to illustrate an analytic procedure.[6]

Columns 7 and 8, respectively, show the involuntarily unemployed and available labor units per family by landholding class. The figures are calculated on Wu and Lee's assumption that the rate of utilization in the ninth group, i.e., 76.99 per cent, is the bench mark from which deviations are measured. When the labor utilization rate falls below 76.99 per cent, as happened in all landholding sizes from one to eight inclusive, involuntary unemployment is considered to have taken place in these groups. The percentage of the extent of involuntary unemployment is measured by the difference between 76.99 per cent and the lower percentage figure of labor utilization in all groups below the ninth. Such figures (difference in percentage) are shown in Column 6. Column 8 is arrived at by multiplying the percentage figure in Column 6 by the potential labor units per farm family in Column 3. When the actual labor utilization figure per farm family (Column 4) is subtracted from the available units of labor in Column 8, the result is units of involuntarily unemployed, as shown in Column 7.[7] We find that unemployment, on the average, is higher for each household in the small landholding class than in the large ones until it completely disappears in households with holdings larger than 4.0 chia (in the ninth group and above).

It is to be noted that off-farm employment reduces the rural unemployment only to a minor extent. Wu and Lee concluded that off-farm jobs are limited, so limited that getting a job which requires no special skill is largely a question of the availability of opportunity.[8] Skilled jobs are available, but most of the farm laborers are not equipped for them. This may have accounted for the rather evenly distributed number of off-farm workers (with one exception) from various landholding intervals. Expressed in percentage of available labor, off-farm work was high at both ends of the landholding classes obviously for entirely different types of work. At the low end, farmers lacking training will mostly get unskilled odd jobs in adjacent areas, whereas relatively well-to-do farmers at the high end of the landholding class have acquired skill through education and usually land on better paid positions. More on the subject of education and off-farm job opportunities will be said in the next section.

On the basis of the present survey, rural unemployment is estimated at about 19 per cent of the total (potential) labor units and 24 per cent of the available labor supply in the early 1960's in Taiwan. This does not mean that such people can be entirely removed without affecting the output because of the seasonal nature of farm activity,[9] as shown in Chapter 3, nor are they necessarily idle. On the farm in Taiwan, the labor force largely consists of members of the family (or extended family). Since the total working units are from one family, work units can be rotated on a certain basis among all members of the family. It is a scheme of two or three persons sharing one job. As a result, each member is busy at a certain season of the year or time of the day. Statistically, we do not find a group identifiable as unemployed on the farm as in the city where no such job-sharing plan is feasible. In this sense, nearly every able-bodied person works and contributes to the total output, yet, when one divides the output of one job-holder by, say, three persons, the marginal output of each would indeed be low.[10] Therefore, one may consider that either all three persons are in a state of disguised unemployment (in J. Robinson's terminology) or two are unemployed (or belong to the disguised unemployment group under some definition). For our present purpose, we call the two persons in the understudy status "unemployed" in order to avoid the confusion of using the term "disguised unemployed."

To analyze one at a time those factors through which land reform affects unemployment on the farm, in Figure 3 we measure on the vertical axis the class interval of land-holdings and on the horizontal axis, labor units. The total and available labor units per family (Columns 3 and 8) are plotted as S_1 and S_2. Both are supply curves in the sense that MVP (price) of labor goes up as the holding size increases (see footnote 6). We label S_1 as the "potential supply" of labor and S_2 as the "available supply." Take any point in a class interval. The horizontal distance between S_1 and S_2 is what we may call voluntary unemployment, the size of which is calculated from the labor utilization figures in Column 5 on the assumption that 23.01 per cent (100 per cent–76.99 per cent) in each class interval are voluntarily unemployed.

D_1 is the average labor utilization per family curve based on the figures in Column 4. It coincides with S_2 at b, which marks the point at which labor utilization reaches the highest point of all class intervals, i.e., 76.99 per cent of the total labor supply in that interval. By previous assumption, all available supply of labor in each of the following intervals is utilized from this interval on. The horizontal distance between D_1 and S_2, appropriately weighted by the size of each interval, measures the unemployment on the farm. The portion where D_1 and S_2 coincide indicates full utilization of available labor at that class interval.

We shall discuss the consequence of land reform on unemployment in terms of possible shifts of these curves.

Increase of Land Productivity

Pursuant to the result of Chapter 5, one may argue that land reform also tends to encourage more initiative on the part of the owner-cultivators to accept new technology and invest more capital in land, thereby making the size of holding less of a restriction. To make it more explicit, we assume that the new technology is land-saving and labor-intensive. For our purpose of illustration, land productivity is affected as if the landholding in each class interval has moved up to the next larger interval, insofar as land is a limitation in the utilization

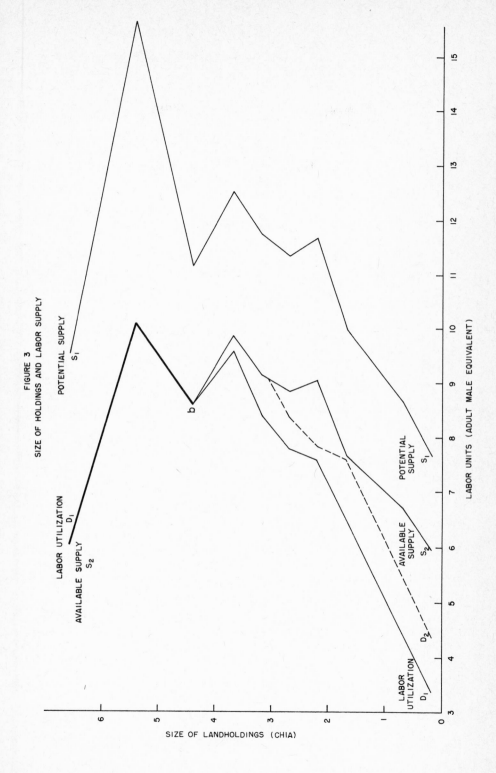

FIGURE 3
SIZE OF HOLDINGS AND LABOR SUPPLY

of labor. For example, labor utilization in the second interval will be 532.23 instead of 422.26 units of labor, in the third interval, 635.04 instead of 532.23, etc. The over-all effect in terms of the graph is a horizontal shift of curve D_1 to the right by one class interval and is illustrated by D_2. Since the distance between D_1 and S_2 represents unemployment on the farm, increase of land productivity following land reform has the effect of reducing the unemployment gap which will now be measured by the distance between D_2 and S_2.

Out-Migration from Agriculture

The role of land reform in expediting labor mobility from the farm will be explored later in this chapter. At this juncture, we shall illustrate the way in which unemployment on the farm will be affected. The estimated available labor on the farm includes both on-farm and off-farm labor. Out-migration of workers from farms can come about in two ways, or a combination of them.

First, assume that the out-migrants are from the pool of those voluntarily unemployed when they were on the farm and they have now moved to the cities. The effect of the out-migration is to shift curve S_1 to the left in the diagram (not shown) with no effect on the unemployment figure. A second possible source is that the out-migration cuts into the available labor supply, or a shift to the left of curve S_2 (not drawn). The reduction of the available labor supply reduces farm unemployment. In a realistic situation, of course, we should expect the out-migrants to come from both potential labor supply and available labor on the farm, and the distribution of out-migrants from the various landholding class intervals may be quite uneven and disproportionate. Qualitatively, a significant factor in the analysis is the possible dynamic effect of out-migration on the agricultural sector. A reduction in the available labor supply on the farm may not affect the normal operation of the farm, yet the seasonal need of labor can only be partially met. Consequently, some modification of crops and farming practices must follow to accommodate the new labor conditions. The implications of such changes cannot be ignored, but are difficult to assess in quantitative terms.

The immediate impact of land reform on unemployment on the farm in Taiwan can be summarized. As shown in Chapter 5, land reform tends to encourage initiative on the part of cultivators to accept new technology and make more capital investment, thereby leading to an increase of productivity of land. This would make possible the absorption of more labor on the farm. In the long run, only out-migration will favorably affect unemployment on the farm in a significant way. To what extent land reform will cause this movement will be the topic of the next section.

LABOR MOBILITY

The problem of transferring surplus labor to urban industrial areas has deserved and received growing attention. In the context of such discussions, it is generally assumed that there is no difference of labor capacity between the agricultural and nonagricultural sectors.[11] Emphasis has accordingly been placed on the wage differentials, the cost of living, and disparity of living conditions in the city, countryside, and so on.

If the hypothesis is indeed true that rural labor has the same capacity as the city workers, the use of capital per worker may account for some difference in the net product per person in the agricultural and nonagricultural sectors, but certainly not to the extent observed in Taiwan. According to the data for 1951-61 in Taiwan, the net per capita income of labor in the agricultural sector has been about one third of the industrial sector and half of the commercial sector and others.[12] Undoubtedly this difference explains in good measure the cause of rural out-migration, i.e., the flow of the relatively low paid farm workers from the agricultural sector to urban and industrial areas. However, given time for dissemination of information on job opportunities and living conditions in urban centers, competition on the supply side of labor should have closed such enormous gaps. Accordingly, one must turn some attention to the possible difference in skills between farm and industrial workers.

What the experience in Taiwan can contribute is that the land reform has wrought a lasting change on the capacity of farm labor by increasing farm income and thereby reducing the financial barrier to education with the consequent increase of rural labor mobility to industry.

Many young people have moved to the cities in recent years.[13] Since only 8 per cent of the civilian men interviewed came as refugees from the mainland, the bulk of the new arrivals in the cities was presumably from the farms. The characteristics of the labor movement formed the subject of a 1961 survey of a total of 520 families selected at random from ten townships, five of which lie in the agricultural districts, two in industrial, and three in mining districts. The nature of movement is defined to include commuters, seasonal workers, and long-term employees. Of the 520 farm families interviewed, 432 families, or 83 per cent, had out-migrating family members.

For the present purpose, we are interested in the nature of labor movement in terms of landownership. When the moving rates of tenants, half-owner-cultivators and owner-cultivators are computed on the basis of the same farm size, the ranking of the three classes in the declining order of moving rates is owner-cultivators, half-owner-cultivators, and tenants. In order to understand why owner-cultivators or half-owner-cultivators as such should have a higher moving rate, we need to look into their qualifications for finding jobs in the cities.

When we classify the number of persons receiving education beyond the sixth grade, by extent of landownership, we find the percentage highest among the owner-cultivators (Table 27), according to the *Report on the 1955 and 1960 Agricultural Census.* As an illustration, in 1955, 80 persons out of 1000 owner-cultivator households graduated from agricultural school or high school, while the comparable figures for half-owner-cultivators and tenants are 55 and 37, respectively. Comparing only the owner-cultivators and tenants, the former is more than double the latter. The gap is closed in 1960, i.e., 189 to 101. When we examine the educational levels of the out-migrants, the noneducated group has the lowest out-migration rate. The rate increases invariably with the level of education for over-all out-migrants and is especially marked with long-term employees. For examples, in Table 28, 85 per cent of those who had not received any education stayed home. For those with a primary education, 60 per cent stayed home. For junior high, 40 per cent stayed on the farm, for senior high about 4 per cent. No one stayed behind after a college education. The generalization is again illustrated by the percentage of out-migrants for various levels of commuters and long-term employees. However, the trend is

Table 27
Number of Persons Receiving Education Beyond Sixth
Grade for Selected Years (Classified by Landownership)
Unit: Number of Persons

| Landownership | Total | Average per 1000 Farm Households | |
		Graduated from Agricultural School	Graduated from High School
Owner-cultivators			
1955	80	23	57
1960	189	27	164
Half-owner-cultivators			
1955	55	20	35
1960	184	25	159
Tenants			
1955	37	10	27
1960	101	10	91

Source: *Basic Statistics of Agricultural Labor and Employment in Taiwan*
(JCRR, Rural Economic Division, Feb.,1963), Table II.

not so obvious for seasonal workers because of the difference
in the nature of jobs in which they are engaged. Most of the
long-term employees were skilled laborers and enjoyed a high
earning capacity. The types of jobs they had, in the order of
frequency were: skilled laborers in factories, salesmen, clerks,
and small businessmen, etc. The same skills were required
of government employees and others who achieved professional
status in the cities. Their average annual income exceeded
NT$10,000. The commuter jobs were confined to adjacent areas.
The types of jobs ranged widely from unskilled to skilled with
monthly income from NT$200 to NT$2,000. Compared with
long-term employees and commuters, most of the seasonal
workers were engaged in unskilled labor, particularly in the
agricultural and mining districts, in which more than 60 per
cent of the seasonal workers were farm laborers. They fared
no better as roadside peddlers, carpenters, etc., in the industrial districts, with average monthly income less than NT$200.
Therefore, seasonal workers were predominantly primary-
school graduates or those with no education. Since only a skilled
laborer can land a long-term job in the cities and it takes

Table 28

Educational Level of Out-Migrants

Unit: Number of persons

Education Level	Total	Stayed Home	Seasonal Worker	Commuter	Long-term Employee	Total	Percentages				
							Stayed Home	Seasonal Worker	Commuter	Long-term Employee	
No education	1058	904	113	25	16	100	85.4	10.7	2.4	1.5	
Primary school	1362	818	270	170	104	100	60.1	19.8	12.4	7.7	
Junior (secondary school)	83	33	8	13	29	100	39.8	9.6	15.7	34.9	
Senior (secondary school)	26	1	....	6	19	100	3.8	...	23.1	73.1	
College	2	...	...		2	100	....	...	....	100	
Total	2531	1756	391	214	170	100	69.4	15.4	8.5	6.7	

Source: T. H. Lee, *A Case Study of Rural Labor Mobility in Relation to Industrialization and Urbanization in Taiwan* (Taipei: JCRR, July, 1962), p. 15.

schooling to learn a skill, it is natural to expect that the percentage of those on the farm who move out on a long-term basis seems to go up with each level of education. But the way land reform seems to play a part in influencing farm workers to get an education remains to be demonstrated.

It is true that the policy of compulsory education for children over six years of age for a period of from four to six years, was initiated when the island was under the control of Japan. But the policy was carried out only among the Japanese nationals on the island. As early as 1917, more than 95 per cent of the school-aged Japanese children attended the grade schools. The percentage reached 99.6 in 1943. For the other residents of Taiwan, the approach to compulsory education for all school-aged children was gradual. Only 13.1 per cent of the Taiwanese school-aged children went to school in 1917. Although the percentage moved up yearly, it never came close to the 99.6 per cent of the Japanese children. At the time of the last available count before the restoration of Taiwan to China, it was 71.3 per cent. The rise of this percentage to 96 within a ten-year period is a spectacular achievement. Since urban people in Taiwan, as a whole, have had more education than the rural people, and since the bulk of the island population lives on the farm, the substantial increase of the percentage of school-aged children receiving compulsory education must be accounted for by the rise of the enrollment in rural schools.

In 1952, a survey was made of 1,176 rural households. The section on education is worth quoting in full because it points to the importance of the economic factor in holding back students at the grade-school level:

Although there is a compulsory attendance law, practically nowhere was it found to be enforced. The reasons for non-enforcement of attendance are several. First of all, attendance is looked upon as a family matter. Non-attendance seems to be centered largely upon economic conditions.... According to local reports, many households can hardly afford to send their children to school for they are thought to be needed at home to help make a living, particularly for the caring of the water buffalo, and other light farm work, and the tending of babies and toddlers.

Some parents cited the cost of proper clothing and of school supplies as a reason for keeping children at home.[14]

In a follow-up study in 1959, the report concluded that:

In rural Taiwan as a whole it would appear that between 93% to 95% of the children in the appropriate age-groups attended elementary school.[15] The desire of rural families to have their children attend school has considerably developed in the last few years. Everyone strongly desired that all children should have at least elementary education. The motives specified are interesting; they were as follows, in order of frequency:

1. people's own experience of 'suffering through illiteracy and ignorance.'

2. improved living conditions since the land reform (making it both more feasible to have the working people educated) .... [16]

In sum, it must be noted that the most significant and universal advance made in rural Taiwan in recent years has been in this field of education. In every township investigated, primary-school attendance rose from 90% in 1952 to between 93% and 95% in 1958. Formerly, many of the parents had to be called upon, reminded, and even threatened, to send their children to school; now they themselves take the initiative and press for admission as soon as possible....

A higher proportion of parents than before feel ashamed if they cannot put their children through secondary school and college. This aspiration is largely social, but realistic calculations are stressed at the same time: both parents and children think that elementary education is insufficient to enable a person to secure employment at a higher level than working on the family farm or in a village shop.[17]

These goals are not merely aspirations. They have been translated into actions, as illustrated by the percentage of primary-school graduates enrolled in secondary schools. If free grade-school education together with some rigid enforcement of the compulsory education law may have explained the rise of enrollment in the primary (grade) schools, they cannot possibly explain the rise of the percentage of primary-school graduates enrolled in junior secondary schools. The latter is neither free nor compulsory. In the 1949-50 academic year, the percentage of primary-school graduates enrolled in junior secondary schools was less than 35 per cent; in 1961-62, it was 52 per cent. Similarly, the percentage of junior secondary-school graduates enrolled in senior secondary schools was 56 per cent in 1949-50, and rose to 82 per cent in 1961-62. The increase since 1949 has been very consistent. The percentage of secondary-school graduates enrolled in the colleges has shown no significant increase. However, we have some direct evidence indicating that the number of children of farmer-purchasers receiving all levels of education has been on the rise. The number of these children enrolled in primary schools increased from 140,641 in 1948 to 433,790 in 1961, and those in the secondary schools increased from 5,380 to 61,523. No one with such a family background entered college in 1948, but 1,602 of them were attending colleges in 1961.[18]

In short, the long-run impact of land reform on farm unemployment undergoes a roundabout process. Briefly stated, the chain reaction starts with more education for children. Since a better trained person will have greater off-farm employability, he is more likely to out-migrate, and, consequently, reduce the farm unemployment. An alternative hypothesis, but compatible with the one suggested in this chapter, is to trace the impact of land reform on farm unemployment through reduction of birth rate. One may argue that more education for rural people will make them more receptive to knowledge about contraception. A reduction of the rural birth rate will no doubt lower the farm labor force and, accordingly, farm unemployment. Unfortunately, lack of data prevents this hypothesis from being tested.[19]

Needless to add, the raising of the educational level of the farmers has also brought about changes for those who choose to remain on the farm. For one thing, education makes them more receptive to accepting new technology. For example, one of the more important technical developments in the post-land reform program is the application of insecticides to rice, sugar cane, fruits, and vegetables. These chemicals are second only to fertilizers in importance to the farmers. The second example is the use of mechanical agricultural implements. The total number of power-tillers was only seven in 1954, but increased to 5,313 in 1961.[20] In a recent comparative study of yields per acre in several countries, covering a period from the mid-1930's to the early 1960's, it was found that one factor facilitating yield increase is a reasonably high level of literacy.[21] In fact, the impact was put in quantitative terms: "Major grain-producing countries with literacy levels below 50 per cent raised yields at 0.2 per cent per year between 1935-39 and 1960-62. Those with literacy levels between 50 and 80 per cent achieved 1.1 per cent annual rate of gain; those above 80 per cent averaged 1.4 per cent."[22] Since such a conclusion is necessarily based on the assumption of *ceteris paribus,* one may not take the above numerical coefficients seriously, yet, the establishment of a positive relation between the level of literacy and the yield in the agricultural sector is an interesting finding.

The rise of education has certainly made the farmers more socially and politically conscious. The number of holders of public offices, such as village, precinct, and neighborhood chiefs; officers of farmers organizations; and members of county or municipal councils; etc., coming from farm families, has doubled or tripled since the land reform.[23] It is a good indication of their drive and desire to take the initiative in economic and related activities, and marks the decline in the almost exclusive leadership of the gentry class, leading to some equalization of social status in rural Taiwan.[24] Some observers considered the establishment and actual implementation of universal primary education in Taiwan the most revolutionary social force in Taiwan which has received the least attention in the outside world, because the achievement of the level of education of the general public makes possible the efficient functioning of the local organizations.[25]

AN ESTIMATE OF OUT-MIGRATION

On the basis of aggregate data, the percentage of agricultural population to total population has a downward trend since 1905. It was 63 per cent in the 1910's, 60 per cent in the 1920's, and 55 per cent in the 1930's.[26] The population of Taiwan increased more rapidly during the 1950's, yet, the downward trend continued until it reached 50 per cent. There is no survey of over-all migration. To determine the order of magnitude of out-migration, a crude estimate will be made by comparing the projected rural population based on its growth rate with the actual.

The net growth rate of population in Taiwan is extremely high. For the period 1950-60, it averaged 3.60 per cent per year. However, it is customary for demographers to emphasize the difference between the urban and rural mortality rates. In a recent study, a comparison was made of death rates in five major cities in Taiwan and the remaining sixteen counties.[27] The former was taken as urban and the latter rural. The mortality rates, based on the observation in 1958 for these two types of communities, were 0.805 per cent for the rural area and 0.575 per cent for the urban, and the difference was found to be statistically significant. Taking the average mortality rate of the two areas as 0.7 per cent, then the rural rate is 0.1 per cent higher than the average rate.

But the rate of natural increase is obtained by taking the difference between the crude birth and death rates. Thus, in order to get an accurate estimate of the growth in agricultural population that should have occurred had there been no out-migration, account should be taken of the rural-urban difference in crude birth rates as well as crude death rates. However, comparable crude birth rates in urban and rural areas were not available except in the form of fertility rates obtained from a survey in 1957 of 4,810 married women from four districts,[28] i.e., Taipei, a suburb, a fishing village, and a farming village. The selection was made to show the urban type of settlement for the first two districts and the rural type for the remaining two. There is a separate category of data for women from mainland China.[29] For our present purpose, we are not really concerned with the actual crude birth rates in the urban and rural areas, but with their difference. This being the case, we take the urban-rural difference in fertility rates as an approximation to their difference in crude birth rates.

Using the adjusted net growth rate of 4.0 per cent per year in the rural area,[30] we estimate the annual increase of the agricultural population in Table 29. The estimated figure for each year is arrived at by multiplying the growth rate and the actual population figure of the immediate preceding year

Table 29
Estimated Number of Out-Migrants
from Agriculture, 1949-59
Unit: 1,000 persons

Year	(1) Actual Agricultural Population	(2) Estimated Population	(3) Out-Migrants from Agriculture	(4) Percentage of Employment to Population (Age 12 and over)	(5) Employment in Non-agricultural Sector
1949	3,899	...			
1950	3,998	4,055	57	37.7	21.5
1951	4,161	4,158	-3	36.6	-1.1
1952	4,257	4,327	70	36.1	25.3
1953	4,382	4,427	45	35.0	15.8
1954	4,489	4,557	68	34.3	23.3
1955	4,603	4,669	66	33.3	22.0
1956	4,699	4,787	88	32.1	28.2
1957	4,790	4,887	97	32.1	31.1
1958	4,881	4,982	101	31.7	32.0
1959	4,975	5,076	101	31.5	31.8
Sum			690		229.9

Source: *Taiwan Statistical Data Book* (1962).

(Column 2). When the estimate is compared with the actual for each year, we will find a difference which can be inferred as in-migration or out-migration from agriculture, depending upon whether the estimated figure is less or greater than the observed. Except for the year 1951, the estimated population based on the growth rate is more than the actual.[31] We account for the difference as out-migration from agriculture. Viewing the period as a whole, the cumulative net out-migrants are about 690,000 persons or 69,000 persons a year, on the average. Expressing the annual figure as a percentage of the agricultural population, out-migration constituted slightly less than 1.5 per cent.

Some of the out-migrants were dependents. In terms of employment, the number should be much less than the migration figure. The ratio of employment to population for Taiwan got smaller every year during the period and was roughly in the range of one third. A detailed yearly estimate is listed in Column 5 of Table 28; the total employed out-migrants for the period was 230,000 persons, averaging 23,000 persons a year. It constituted about 1.5 per cent of the nonagricultural labor force. The estimate may have been a conservative one because the age distribution of the out-migrants was highly in favor of those in the active labor force, and in evaluating the figures, we must recognize the importance of such out-migration to marginal workers in the population, most of whom were firmly attached to the farm. Nevertheless, the total is modest. On this score, the immediate effect of land reform is disappointing because in the countries where per capita income grew significantly, the proportion of the labor force engaged in agriculture declined and that engaged in nonagriculture industries increased, and the shifts have been quite marked.[32]

SUMMARY AND CONCLUSION

A sample survey of farm employment was used to focus our attention on the need to use an operational definition of unemployment on the farm in our examination of the impact of land reform on farm employment. The short-run consideration of increase of land productivity may reduce farm unemployment to some extent. However, only such forces as the raising of the educational level of the average farmer and the acceptance of new farm technology will have any long-run effects. In the last analysis, short of substantial out-migration from agriculture in Taiwan, where the pressure of population in relation to land is high, there is little prospect of reducing farm unemployment. So far, the number of net out-migrants is still too small to have a noticeable effect on the unemployment picture. The result may be somewhat unexpected in view of the substantial difference in the per capita income of labor in agriculture and the factories. As argued in this chapter, training and minimum education still are prerequisites to obtaining employment in the industries. It takes time and some investment on the part of farm workers to get them. A higher wage rate in the nonagricultural sector serves as a useful stimulant in the short run, but in the long run, only those who meet the qualifications of employment in the cities can answer the call and stay on the job.

CHAPTER 8 — COSTS OF LAND REFORM

The discussion in the previous chapters has been confined to the impact and consequences of land reform. In the present chapter, we shall dwell upon the cost of land reform as an instrument of policy for economic development. In order to determine whether land reform should be adopted, it is necessary to assess the net benefit of implementing such a program, however imperfect it may be. It is only by weighing the costs and gains, one can say, that we have learned the lesson from the experience. Two aspects of the costs will be considered, namely, the money cost of implementing land reform and the opportunity cost of emphasizing the expansion of agriculture versus the establishment of industries. The markets for the potential new industries created by an expansion of the agricultural output will also be examined. On the other hand, we shall not consider social, and possibly other noneconomic, costs as we have not included gains from such sources in the discussion either.

MONEY COST

Taking stock of the money cost of land reform is one way of finding how efficiently land reform measures have been implemented by the various units of government. Such a task of evaluation would hardly be possible had it not been for the unique role of JCRR in implementing land reform in Taiwan, which can be easily singled out for scrutiny and for the accessibility of its receipts and expenditures.

The Sino-American Joint Commission was organized in the fall of 1948 with the objective of assisting the Chinese Government to increase agricultural production and improve the living conditions of the rural people. The commission's

principles of operation were largely worked out on the mainland of China during the ten months following the creation
of the agency. The program in Taiwan was begun in April,
1949, and developed on a comprehensive basis after the
headquarters of the commission moved to Taipei in the fall
of the same year. From 1949 to 1953, JCRR made important
recommendations which finally materialized in the establishment of a system of regional supervision of the 37.5 per cent
rent limitation program, the reorganization of the farm tenancy committees on the various levels, and the vigorous
execution of the public land sales program. The general
landownership classification of 1951, the construction of
facilities for storing cadastral maps and records in 1954,
and the inspection and thorough rechecking in 1954 of farm
families who had purchased either public land or private
tenanted land have been carried out mostly on the initiative
and recommendation of JCRR. JCRR also contributed a full
share to the drafting, discussion, and final adoption of the
Land-to-the-Tiller Act and Regulations Governing the Issuance
of Land Bonds in Kind, both of which involved the people's
rights and obligations and affected the success or failure of
the land reform program as a whole.[1]

The money from JCRR for the land reform was timely
and served as a catalyst for many projects. The major
item of support by JCRR in land reform has been the land-
to-the-tiller program. Next are its supports for the 37.5
per cent rent reduction and, to a relatively minor extent, the
sale of public land.[2] In addition to appropriations for land
reform, JCRR is instrumental in channeling United States aid
funds to agricultural development. A complete list of JCRR
appropriations from 1950 to 1961 is shown in Table 30.
There are two parts to the appropriations, one is in local
currency and the other in U.S. dollars, which, according to
the JCRR report, were used to cover the cost of equipment
and supplies imported in connection with irrigation and crop
production projects. The scope covered is quite comprehensive
and mostly consists of supplementary measures to land reform,
such as rural health, fisheries, live-stock production, etc.
In fact, the largest item, water use and control, at NT$85
million, is almost three times that of the next item, budget
support to local agricultural programs, at NT$31 million. Of the
total budget for eleven years, the administrative expenses
consist of NT$15 million, which is slightly less than 6 per
cent of the total.

Table 30
JCRR Allocation of Money for Major Categories, 1950-61
Unit: $1,000
Fiscal Year 1950-61

Activity	New Taiwan Dollars* (constant 1949)	U.S. Dollars
Crop production	29,933.0	1,027.2
Livestock production	10,426.5	348.9
Water use and control	84,688.3	2,402.1
Forestry and soil conservation	14,575.7	457.3
Rural organization and agricultural extension	13,695.2	88.0
Economic research and agricultural credit	26,646.2	11.4
Fisheries	12,034.7	30.5
Land reform	4,421.7	...
Rural health	10,648.1	317.5
Agricultural research and education	8,102.8	643.0
Rural electrification and communication	4,561.6	...
Government budget support to local agricultural programs	30,857.8	1,027.0
Miscellaneous projects	9,005.6	158.0
Administration	15,196.0	304.7
	274,793.9	6,815.6

*Expenses are listed by year in current NT$. In view of fluctuations of the value of currency, additions over the years can only be meaningful in 1949 constant NT$. Accordingly, the current NT$ figures were deflated by a price index with 1949 = 100.

Source: *Twelfth General Report of the JCRR* (Taipei: JCRR, 1961).

The wide range of JCRR activities is in line with the basic philosophy under which JCRR operated, as set forth by the late Chairman Monlin Chiang. He said that the program of the commission was designed to assist in achieving two fundamental principles, social justice (i.e., fair distribution) and material well-being (i.e., increase of production), and that the commission attempted to strike a balance between these two programs because working for social justice alone would achieve but an equalization of poverty, whereas working for increased production alone would widen the gap between the have's and have-not's. Although the implementation of the land reform program was mentioned so far as the more important contribution of JCRR, the equally challenging task of increasing material well-being through greater production has been met by the commission with the same zeal and devotion.

In order not to lose sight of the more tangible dividend from those projects indirectly related, we shall mention them in passing by way of a few examples.

In the case of rice breeding, continuous research supported by JCRR has produced Chianung 242, a heavy yielder and resistant variety of record. A number of promising lines are being developed by the experimental stations in Taichung, Chiayi, and Pingtung. A few of them possess a higher level of blast resistance than Chianung 242.

The main upland food crops grown in Taiwan are sweet potatoes, peanuts, soybeans, wheat, and corn. Their combined cultivation acreage exceeds 400,000 hectares a year. Except for wheat and some soybeans, which are grown principally in paddy fields following the harvesting of the second rice crop during the winter, the others are planted largely in dry land with no irrigation water or application of fertilizer. The increase in the productivity of the dry-land crops was made largely by introducing many new varieties through the combined efforts of JCRR, local agricultural research and improvement stations, farmers' associations, and government offices. Recently, an improved method was developed by the Taichung District Agricultural Improvement Station. The method is to remove every fourth row of rice seedlings and have half of them transplanted on the third row and the rest on the fifth row, thus leaving a space for the interplanting of sweet potato vines. With the provision of this planting row, the sweet potato vines can be interplanted in the paddy fields twenty to twenty-five days earlier than under the conventional method. The new method was tried in 1960, and the result showed that the average increase in yield over the conventional method was 56 per cent in tubers and 45 per cent in potato vines.

Agricultural extension in Taiwan is largely a teaching process, but its methods are different from those of the classroom. It makes full use of audio-visual aids, but it depends basically on demonstrations of methods by extension workers and demonstrations of results by farmers on their own farms and in their homes. The work is carried on in three-way cooperation among the Provincial Department of Agriculture and Forestry, the Provincial Farmers' Association, and JCRR. Under the arrangement, the PDAF is the sponsoring agency and PFA, the executing agency. JCRR provides financial and technical assistance and guidance at all levels. Extension with adult farmers was started in 1955. By 1960, it had covered 277 of the 317 agricultural townships in Taiwan.

Turning to the expenditures incurred by the various levels of government for land reform, we examine the provincial budget and the budgets of the counties and the villages. There was no explicit item except for one entitled "economic development expenses." Such expenses at the provincial level are largely devoted to the irrigation projects, including the utilization of underground water resources, development of forestry, expansion of harbor facilities, improvement of the highway system, and construction of low-cost housing for civil service employees. A separate listing of irrigation subsidies and investment showed great yearly variations as a percentage of the total. No details are available for the development expenses at the county and village levels, and they are presumably devoted to similar purposes. We have no way to determine the proportion that is devoted to the implementation of land reform or agricultural development, and the aggregate can only be taken as a rough approximation to such expenses. The total of such expenses each year at the three levels of government is relegated to the footnote.[3] The year-to-year fluctuation is somewhat exaggerated by the changing value of the new Taiwan dollar. In terms of the constant 1949 new Taiwan dollar, the total spent under the item amounts to NT$587 million. The peak years were 1952 and 1953, when the land-to-the-tiller program was put into effect. It has since levelled off at NT$50 million a year, a figure approximating the average for the entire twelve-year period. To this, one must add private investment in irrigation projects by its irrigation association. The amount was clearly accountable, and over the period 1949-60, a sum of NT$84.3 million (in 1949 price) was spent.

All told, a decade of implementation of land reform and agriculture cost JCRR $6.8 million (U.S. dollars) and NT$275 million, the government NT$587 million, and the irrigation associations with their contributions to irrigation projects, NT$84 million, making a grand total of $6.8 million (U.S. dollars) and NT$946 million (in 1949 new Taiwan dollars).

OPPORTUNITY COST: ESTABLISHMENT
OF INDUSTRIES VERSUS EXPANSION OF AGRICULTURE

The record shows that what was required for larger agricultural output during the period was better organization and better methods of production. Improvement on these lines involved a land reform program (broadly defined), i.e., a rationalization of holdings, an intensive program of agricultural research, a good extension service, equitable distribution of yield between the owner and the tenant, a tax and subsidy scheme giving incentive to increase output, and some credit facilities on reasonable terms. On the other hand, industrial projects as a whole require much capital equipment. In view of the limited resources of the island for the manufacture of capital equipment, Taiwan, as in other underdeveloped areas, will have to import a large portion of such equipment. The question of capital provision is consequently not merely a matter of savings; it is also a problem of the balance of payments. It is not possible to suppose that the difficulty can be overcome, to more than a very limited extent, by the inflow of external capital. The amount of capital accumulation that can be financed from the domestic saving is liable to be more limited than would be apparant from the consideration of saving potential alone.[4]

A shortage of foreign exchange was an acute economic problem facing Taiwan. There was a deficit on its trade account every year for 1950-61, the period under consideration. The deficit ran from $30 million (U.S. dollars) in 1950 to $110 million (U.S. dollars) in 1961. The chief financial source used to meet the deficit has been U.S. aid. In 1961, the aid was $108 million (U.S. dollars),[5] covering almost the entire deficit on the trade account.

In minimizing the strain on the balance of payments, we are only looking at one aspect of the contribution of the investment in land reform; the other side of the contribution should be measured in terms of the earnings of foreign exchange from the export proceeds of its agricultural products and indirectly through processed agricultural commodities. Annual exports of the agricultural products ranged from $7 million (U.S. dollars) in 1950 to $40 million in 1955, and the processed agricultural products, from $63 million in 1951 to $125 million in 1957. Expressing the export proceeds of the agricultural and processed agricultural products in the percentage of the total, it was 18.6 per cent, on the average, for the former and 66.7 per cent for the latter in the period of twelve years.

Those who believe that the savings devoted to the land reform programs could have served the cause of development faster by having been channeled to industrial projects instead, have oversimplified the problem. There is hidden in such contentions the implicit assumption that all investment projects have the same proportion of investment in imports. The assumption is arbitrary, and contrary to the experience in Taiwan. Once the balance of payments can be eased, not temporarily, but as a long-run trend, by an expansion of agricultural output, the process of industrialization would be expedited.

It is true that the above comparison is based on the criterion of balance of payments only. There is the larger question of weighing the over-all contribution of agriculture versus industry to the economic development, and the literature on the subject is extensive.

But the discussion seems to have been clouded by a lack of a more clear-cut agreement on the economic goal, because the real issue is what types of policies will do the best job of raising per capita income given the limited resources at a country's disposal.

It may be true that priority on agriculture will maximize the present income, which in turn will lead to higher income in the future. On the other hand, one may argue that by taking a lower income than would have been achieved under the comparative marginal-productivity approach, a country can nevertheless attain a stream of higher future income through emphasizing industrial development at the initial stage.

Putting the difference between the two approaches in this manner, several questions may be raised. First, would the course of action emphasizing the establishment of industries necessarily lead to a stream of income higher than from the expansion of agriculture? A higher income stream from a certain point on is no guarantee of an improvement of the well-being of the people. Much depends on the intertemporal utility of present versus future income. It is true that we may compare two streams of income by discounting each to the present value. However, the procedure is not a simple one. There is the difference between borrowing and lending rates, the problem of varying rates depending on the amount borrowed,6 and the imperfection of capital markets in the underdeveloped countries with a simultaneous existence of a host of interest rates in various regions based on types of assets provided as security for the loan.

Even if one can achieve a higher discounted income through the industry-first policy, there is the question of uncertainty over the future. It is a problem to which little or no attention has been paid in development discussions. In a few restricted cases, it is possible to construct some certainty equivalent to the probability distribution of outcomes from a given course of actions. But many actions will be undertaken in the presence of uncertainty that would never be undertaken in the face of any possible set of certain alternatives. For example, a producer uncertain of the demand for his products in the future will tend to install a plant designed for flexibility of a type that he would never consider if he knew in advance just exactly what the size and character of his sales would be.

In Taiwan, there was no evidence of competition for skilled labor or entrepreneurs between the agricultural and industrial sectors. The special skills or entrepreneurship that were needed for industries were wanting on the farm; nor could the farm sector make effective use or pay for such talents if they were available. In Chapter 4, we noted that a few ex-landlords had succeeded in becoming entrepreneurs; and it was also found in Chapter 7 that out-migrants from the farm were limited in number and confined to a small group of educated ones. Few out-migrated from the farm, not so much because they were needed on the farm as because they were not adequately prepared to land a permanent job in the industrial sector. If the farm and industry were indeed drawing on two noncompeting groups of workers and entrepreneurs, and the competition for land input between them is usually minimal, the opportunity cost of a land reform in Taiwan was negligible. Thus, in the last analysis, the foreign exchange resources (measured by the initial outlays, parts for normal upkeep, imported raw materials for keeping the plants running, and export proceeds) constitute the major effective constraint in making the initial choice between various investment alternatives. On that score, land reform seemed to have exerted less of a strain on the balance of payments than industrial development would for the period under consideration.

There is another aspect to the thesis that the opportunity cost of land reform is low. Suppose we broaden the conventional definition of capital as suggested by Kuznets. If by capital formation we mean the use of any current resources that add to future output, certainly significant fractions of outlays incurred by the owner-cultivators on the education of their children, improvement of their health, and even on living, insofar as they contribute to the greater productivity, should be included under capital. Then, a broader base of economic development has been laid by the land reform than we realize in view of the size of the rural population affected. In fact Kuznets went further. According to him, the need for physical stock of capital can be met "by substituting training and education of human beings and the improvement in the whole fabric of social organization for machines."[7] Our mention in passing of the number of holders of public offices coming from farming families (in Chapter 7) is but an instance reflecting on the social change. An evaluation of the extent to which the land reform has improved social organization would certainly go beyond the scope of the present study. The universal acceptance of educational opportunities in rural areas in Taiwan is, however, a fact. In making these comments, we do not deny the importance of physical capital accumulation for economic development, but seek to redress the possible downward bias in assessing the contribution of the land reform to capital formation.

MARKETS FOR NEW INDUSTRIES CREATED BY EXPANSION OF AGRICULTURE

The expansion of agricultural output necessitates some increases of the farm input, including those from the industrial sector. In Taiwan, they were materials consisting chiefly of pesticides and chemical fertilizer (Table 17). A 1957 farm income study shows that farmers spent 22 per cent of their total farm expenditure on fertilizer, which was the largest item of expenditures.[8] Of the total, about two thirds were supplied domestically. Using 1953 as the base, the aggregate index measuring the use of industrial products as inputs in agriculture stood at 137 in 1959. The change was, however, not monotonic; there was a decline in the years 1954 and 1955.[9]

The farmers' purchases of household goods from the non-agricultural sector also rose (Table 16). In terms of 1935-37

Taiwan dollars, total consumption by the farm sector of non-farm products was T$120 million in 1950, T$187 million in 1955, and T$253 million in 1960—more than doubling in a decade. If adjustments were made for more serious underestimation in the early 1950's, the increase over the decade might not be so impressive, but would be still considerable. The increase is attributable partly to the rise of the farm family income from T$276 million (in 1935-37 Taiwan dollars) in 1950, to T$378 million in 1955, to T$577 million in 1960, and partly to a change of the percentage distribution of consumption expenditure between the farm and nonfarm products. In 1950, the farm families divided their consumption expenditure almost equally between the two sectors, while in 1960 they spent 40 per cent of their total income on farm products, as against 44 per cent on nonfarm products.

Although a precise relationship between an increase of demand for consumers' goods and a concomitant increase of investment through the working of the acceleration principle cannot be firmly established, one must admit the stimulant effect of the expansion of agricultural output in creating markets for the products of potential new industries. To be sure, improvement in the efficiency of agricultural production cannot by itself be the goal of economic development in Taiwan; it should be regarded only as a stepping stone in a situation with certain constraints toward industrialization,[10] in which must rest the ultimate hope for the solution of underemployment and improved level of living in Taiwan. There is no use giving incentive or stimulus to the industrialists unless it is a stimulus to do something which is within their capability. The provision of a basic social and economic framework that permits and induces a substantial rise of the output of the industrial sector should be the other side of the same policy. Under a badly lagging industrial section, even the yield-raising efforts in agriculture may quickly reach the limit.[11]

SUMMARY AND CONCLUSION

In order to assess the result of a social and economic experiment such as land reform in Taiwan, one must look at the cost of such a program, as we attempted to do in this chapter. Admittedly, our figures for the money cost are, at best, rough, and our approach to assessing the opportunity cost crude and inadequate. The discussion will at least give us cause to ponder. In the case of Taiwan, when we add up the money cost of land reform, subject, of course, to the qualifications mentioned in the text, the sum was modest, judging by the result; nor was the opportunity cost too high after weighing the alternatives. At a more fundamental level, the cost-benefit analysis under two conflicting policy desiderata is meaningful if we aim at the same goal or objective. The above accounting of the costs does not pretend to answer the question of what the objective should be. The answer depends on one's value judgment. Therefore, the conclusion in this chapter should be accepted in this light.

CHAPTER **9** SUMMARY AND
CONCLUSION

Land reform in Taiwan, initiated in 1949 and completed in 1953, proceeded in three stages. First was a rent limitation to a maximum of 37.5 per cent of the principal crop. The second stage of the reform began with the sale of government land acquired from the Japanese nationals at the end of World War II. It culminated in the promulgation in 1953 of the Land-to-the-Tiller Act under which the government resold the land compulsorily purchased from the absentee landlords to the tenant-cultivators.

The magnitude of this job can best be illustrated by the number of families affected. Lease contracts that were revised under the new tenancy law totaled 377,000. About 140,000 families bought public land. Of the landlords 106,000 sold their land to the government, which in turn sold it to 195,000 families under the land-to-the-tiller program. Administratively, land reform was by no means a simple and routine operation. The implementation of the program called for the establishment of special agencies such as farm tenancy committees and the training of staff workers. For example, the training was carried out on four different levels of administrative unit: provincial, *hsien* and city, district, and village and township. There were, in addition, the problems of dissemination of information and of educating the public. Equally challenging were such tasks as the appraisal of land value, screening and approval of prospective buyers, compilation of lists of land to be compulsorily purchased, compensation to landlords, collection of first installment from the farmer-purchasers, and handling of disputes. All of these, and many more details, were completed in five years.

The impact of land reform on the Taiwan economy was both immediate and far reaching. Income redistribution through rent limitation was made effective at once, and it is noteworthy that the interests of landlords were reasonably well protected.

A far more important aspect of land reform is the increase of agricultural productivity. Indicators based on aggregate statistics and the data of the major crops (paddy rice, in particular) pointed toward historical heights. It is admitted that the increase cannot be attributed entirely to land reform, in encouraging more intensive application of capital and labor per unit of land by the owner-cultivators. The real issue is, therefore, this: Given the resources and technology of Taiwan in the late 1940's, was agricultural development, with land reform as its first step, the most logical economic policy to follow? Our study found that the resources and technological constraints of Taiwan in the late 1940's were such that land reform did not preclude the economy from developing industrially. There was no evidence of competition for skilled labor or entrepreneurs between the agricultural and industrial sectors; nor was demand for land input from the industrial projects high. Foreign exchange resources constituted the major constraint in making the initial choice between various investment projects. On this score, land reform exerted little strain on the balance of payments. In short, the opportunity cost of land reform and agricultural development was minimal.

Looking at the positive side, we found land reform contributed to the industrial development of Taiwan. Exports related to output from the agricultural sector averaged two thirds of the total exports in the 1950's. There was stimulus to industrial output brought about by the demand for such agricultural inputs as fertilizer and insecticide and by the enlarged demand for consumption goods following the rise of farm income. Many who got the immediate benefit of land reform can believe that there is a relationship between reward and performance. The power of incentive in an economy should never be underestimated. This is evidenced by the prevalent utilization of incremental income on the part of farmers to educate their children. Investment in human capital must be predicated on the belief that children who receive an education will get a reasonable rate of return and that they will get as much of a chance for upward mobility in the society as other children of similar ability. Since education makes possible the fullest and optimum use of human resources, an economic policy that contributes to this end has laid a foundation for a dynamic and productive society.

To conclude, I shall report an interview I had in the summer of 1963 with Dr. Monlin Chiang, the late chairman of JCRR. I asked him what he considered to have been the factors that made major contributions to the outcome of land reform in Taiwan. Dr. Chiang, after minutes of reflection, mentioned three. First, it was the determination of everyone involved in the project to make it work, from the highest person in the government to the field worker. He reminded me of the circumstances under which the land reform was initiated in Taiwan. It was during the difficult period in 1949 when the crossing of the Taiwan Straits by the mainland Communists was thought imminent. Second, he gave credit to such ground-works as the cadastral system and household registration, etc., which were laid during the years that the island was under the control of Japan. These accomplishments saved precious time at a critical juncture. Third, he thanked the United States for the financial support and provision of experts on agricultural technology and production know-how. It is indeed difficult to add to or subtract from what Dr. Chiang had said, but he was understandably too modest to mention the role played by him and JCRR as catalytic agents in harnessing these factors into a winning combination.

STATISTICAL APPENDIX

Table 1

Value of Agricultural Products Deflated by Price Index, 1912-61

(Unit: T$1,000)

Year	(1) Value of Agricultural Products	(2) Income of Agricultural Sector	(3) Price Index (1935-37 = 100)	(4) Population in Agricultural Sector (1,000 persons)	(5) (1) Deflated by Price Index	(6) (2) Deflated by Price Index	(7) (5) Per Capita	(8) (6) Per Capita
1912	92,735	109,064	68.25	2,087*	135,875	159,801	65.1	76.6
1913	100,804	101,142	65.80	2,199	153,197	153,711	69.7	69.9
1914	80,490	67,484	56.01	(2,226)**	143,706	120,485	64.5 66.4	54.1 66.9
1915	76,083	662,944	49.27	(2,253)**	154,421	127,754	68.5	56.7
1916	88,499	71,888	52.94	2,280	167,168	135,791	73.3	59.5
1917	130,637	103,568	69.13	(2,285)**	188,972	149,817	82.7	65.5
1918	175,017	141,520	97.72	(2,291)**	179,100	144,822	78.1	63.2
1919	252,440	183,025	125.55	2,297	201,067	145,778	87.5 78.0	63.4 61.7
1920	201,726	139,135	121.14	(2,262)**	166,523	114,855	73.6	50.7
1921	200,584	140,301	109.89	2,227	182,532	127,674	81.9	57.3
1922	186,258	132,098	87.59	2,220	212,647	150,814	95.7	67.9
1923	192,939	137,675	92.41	2,263	208,785	148,983	92.2	65.8
1924	253,774	181,092	103.68	2,305	244,767	174,665	106.1 89.9	75.7 63.5
1925	308,040	220,476	119.08	2,340	258,683	185,150	110.5	79.1
1926	291,891	211,130	115.09	2,377	253,620	183,448	106.6	77.1
1927	272,441	189,916	103.31	2,402	263,712	183,831	109.7	76.5
1928	293,938	212,280	105.18	2,458	279,462	201,826	113.6	82.1
1929	301,868	218,145	105.77	2,489	285,400	206,244	114.6 111.0	82.8 79.5
1930	259,361	187,906	85.20	2,534	304,414	220,546	120.1	87.0
1931	209,973	151,946	68.12	2,583	308,239	223,057	119.3	86.3
1932	278,963	207,968	92.24	2,576	302,431	225,464	117.4	87.5
1933	237,988	157,347	74.46	2,638	319,618	211,317	121.1	80.1
1934	292,910	207,758	83.91	2,701	349,076	247,596	129.2 121.4	91.6 86.5

Year										
1935	361,046	260,621	96.73	2,790	373,251	269,431	133.7		96.5	
1936	388,266	275,613	100.20	2,855	387,491	275,063	135.7		96.3	
1937	402,996	286,262	103.07	2,880	390,993	277,736	135.7		96.2	
1938	460,213	329,814	112.57	2,896	408,824	292,986	141.1		101.1	
1939	551,826	406,854	134.11	2,925	411,473	303,373	140.6	137.4	103.7	98.8
1940	541,447	389,522	150.94	2,984	358,717	258,064	120.2		86.4	
1941	573,689	433,776	161.49	3,070	355,247	268,608	115.7		87.4	
1942	631,557	501,277	175.68	3,187	359,493	285,335	112.7		89.5	
1943	614,734	487,046	176.45	3,271	348,390	276,025	106.5		84.3	
1944	782,524	576,443	248.82	3,318	314,620	231,764	94.8	110.0	69.8	83.5
1945	831,794	594,541	513.08	3,366	162,118	115,877	48.1		34.4	
1946	38,968,626	32,989,991	16,283.68	(3,494)**	239,311	202,651	68.4		57.9	
1947	1,38,539,063	98,789,443	65,539.00	(3,622)**	211,384	150,732	57.7		41.6	
1948	1,233,758,335	965,601,085	381,002.00	(3,750)**	323,819	253,437	86.3		67.5	
1949	1,531,003	1,179,441	467.80	3,879	327,277	252,125	84.3	69.0	64.9	53.3
1950	2,786,752	1,975,588	738.94	3,998	377,128	267,354	94.3		66.8	
1951	3,812,441	2,660,681	1,040.18	4,161	366,517	255,790	88.0		61.4	
1952	5,837,552	3,937,448	1,380.70	4,257	422,797	285,178	99.3		66.9	
1953	8,681,412	6,292,289	1,824.89	4,382	475,722	344,804	108.5		78.6	
1954	7,430,644	5,265,896	1,503.07	4,489	494,364	350,343	110.1	100.0	78.0	70.3
1955	9,494,860	6,501,216	1,944.47	4,603	488,301	334,344	106.0		72.6	
1956	10,574,045	7,016,138	1,999.74	4,699	528,770	350,853	112.5		74.6	
1957	12,390,940	8,113,576	2,197.26	4,790	563,926	369,259	117.7		77.0	
1958	13,709,273	8,172,744	2,262.68	4,881	605,886	361,198	124.1		74.0	
1959	15,611,830	10,230,959	2,581.69	4,975	604,713	396,289	121.5	116.4	79.6	75.6
1960	20,659,550		3,393.01	5,373						
1961	23,186,683									

* Figure for 1933.
** Interpolated figures.

Sources: (1) *Taiwan Agricultural Yearbook* 1962, p. 28.
        (2) JCRR data.
        (3) *Ibid.*
        (4) *Taiwan Statistical Data Book* (Table 194), p. 23.

Table 2

Brown Rice: Production, Acreage of Plantation, and Output per Hectare, 1900-61

Year	(1) Brown Rice Production (metric tons)			(2) Acreage of Plantation (hectares)			(3) Output per Hectare (kilograms)				
	Total	1st Crop	2nd Crop	Total	1st Crop	2nd Crop	Total	1st Crop	2nd Crop	Paddy	Uplands
1900	307,147	152,098	155,049	325,653	160,463	165,217	943	948	938	966	598
1901	437,977	278,634	159,343	355,360	178,407	174,953	1,239	1,562	911	1,318	485
1902	403,061	222,225	180,836	344,989	162,990	181,999	1,168	1,363	994	1,217	547
1903	525,316	279,977	245,339	394,868	191,704	203,164	1,330	1,460	1,208	1,356	1,085
1904	594,266	302,906	291,360	435,134	197,992	237,142	1,366	1,530	1,229	1,406	1,033
1905	621,978	326,067	295,911	447,432	210,495	236,937	1,390	1,549	1,249	1,418	1,131
1906	566,940	301,943	264,997	458,591	214,789	243,802	1,236	1,406	1,087	1,273	886
1907	644,592	294,475	350,117	471,647	216,810	254,837	1,367	1,358	1,374	1,406	984
1908	665,232	324,117	341,115	478,953	226,497	252,456	1,389	1,431	1,351	1,427	1,010
1909	661,421	341,666	319,755	478,955	224,034	254,921	1,381	1,525	1,254	1,415	946
1910	598,211	301,168	297,043	456,276	212,884	243,392	1,311	1,415	1,220	1,335	990
1911	641,516	344,225	297,291	478,730	217,885	260,895	1,340	1,580	1,140	1,386	840
1912	578,087	299,503	278,584	481,204	217,545	263,659	1,201	1,377	1,057	1,243	779
1913	732,331	369,858	362,473	494,313	224,481	269,832	1,482	1,648	1,343	1,535	959
1914	658,322	284,673	373,649	499,679	224,382	275,297	1,317	1,269	1,357	1,372	801
1915	683,511	324,839	358,672	491,089	223,734	267,355	1,392	1,452	1,342	1,436	933
1916	664,167	353,755	310,412	471,677	215,345	256,332	1,408	1,643	1,211	1,456	867
1917	690,545	350,622	339,923	466,184	210,909	255,275	1,481	1,662	1,332	1,531	920
1918	661,744	344,584	317,160	483,344	212,672	270,672	1,369	1,620	1,172	1,415	884
1919	703,320	344,198	359,122	497,211	224,900	272,311	1,415	1,530	1,319	1,467	902
1920	691,764	339,400	352,364	500,169	222,638	277,531	1,383	1,524	1,270	1,429	900
1921	710,899	358,491	353,408	495,426	220,343	275,083	1,435	1,627	1,281	1,477	922
1922	777,831	390,803	387,028	511,241	228,430	282,811	1,521	1,711	1,369	1,627	891
1923	695,155	371,406	363,669	507,829	224,913	282,916	1,369	1,652	1,144	1,414	788
1924	868,090	425,717	442,373	531,450	234,586	296,864	1,633	1,815	1,490	1,674	1,131
1925	920,452	453,445	467,007	550,835	241,727	309,108	1,671	1,876	1,511	1,725	1,006
1926	887,739	404,589	483,150	567,172	250,163	317,009	1,565	1,617	1,524	1,605	1,041

Year										
1927	985,524	464,930	520,594	585,011	258,497	326,514	1,685	1,799	1,594	1,722	1,165
1928	970,715	456,702	514,013	584,918	261,421	323,497	1,660	1,747	1,589	1,688	1,219
1929	925,824	407,507	518,317	567,952	232,885	335,067	1,630	1,750	1,547	1,666	1,024
1930	1,052,931	497,520	555,411	614,390	267,036	347,354	1,714	1,863	1,599	1,743	1,293
1931	1,068,549	518,349	550,200	633,726	274,352	359,374	1,686	1,889	1,531	1,707	1,364
1932	1,278,459	603,064	675,395	664,325	283,356	380,969	1,924	2,128	1,773	1,955	1,460
1933	1,194,549	562,676	631,873	675,476	286,439	389,037	1,768	1,964	1,624	1,819	1,035
1934	1,298,412	644,435	653,977	666,979	288,475	378,504	1,947	2,234	1,728	1,997	1,205
1935	1,303,164	618,313	684,851	678,629	296,614	382,015	1,920	2,085	1,793	1,962	1,267
1936	1,365,484	676,930	688,554	681,548	301,512	380,036	2,004	2,245	1,812	2,051	1,239
1937	1,319,018	630,228	688,790	657,685	295,203	362,482	2,006	2,135	1,900	2,056	1,150
1938	1,402,414	697,934	704,480	625,398	282,462	342,936	2,242	2,471	2,054	2,292	1,156
1939	1,307,391	575,877	731,514	626,131	267,203	358,928	2,088	2,155	2,038	2,124	1,196
1940	1,128,784	603,378	525,406	638,622	277,811	360,811	1,768	2,172	1,456	1,809	740
1941	1,199,006	597,652	601,354	646,927	292,640	354,287	1,853	2,042	1,697	1,884	1,048
1942	1,171,182	548,404	622,778	616,529	267,800	348,729	1,900	2,048	1,786	1,934	808
1943	1,125,804	546,350	579,454	610,051	271,838	338,213	1,845	2,010	1,713	1,880	547
1944	1,068,121	555,347	512,774	600,688	269,330	331,358	1,778	2,062	1,547	1,808	605
1945	638,828	342,014	296,814	502,018	231,897	270,121	1,273	1,475	1,099	1,289	517
1946	894,021	382,917	511,104	564,016	204,545	359,471	1,535	1,872	1,422	1,617	1,027
1947	999,022	471,419	527,593	677,557	287,395	390,162	1,474	1,640	1,352	1,512	808
1948	1,068,421	513,880	554,541	717,744	311,598	406,146	1,489	1,649	1,365	1,552	625
1949	1,214,523	577,487	637,036	747,675	320,152	427,523	1,624	1,804	1,490	1,684	818
1950	1,421,486	678,004	743,482	770,262	336,957	433,305	1,845	2,012	1,716	1,909	1,011
1951	1,434,792	716,326	768,466	789,075	346,518	442,557	1,882	2,067	1,736	1,944	1,087
1952	1,570,115	757,289	812,826	785,729	346,718	437,011	1,998	2,172	1,860	2,071	988
1953	1,641,557	740,124	901,433	778,384	344,264	434,120	2,109	2,150	2,076	2,174	1,104
1954	1,695,107	836,452	858,655	776,660	353,636	423,024	2,183	2,365	2,030	2,271	807
1955	1,614,953	711,305	903,648	750,739	306,185	444,554	2,151	2,323	2,033	2,215	1,045
1956	1,789,829	906,724	883,105	783,629	339,395	444,234	2,234	2,672	1,988	2,353	863
1957	1,839,009	931,699	907,310	783,267	346,454	436,813	2,348	2,689	2,077	2,408	893
1958	1,894,127	934,027	960,100	778,189	344,032	434,157	2,434	2,715	2,211	2,486	1,053
1959	1,856,316	930,233	926,083	776,050	341,432	434,618	2,392	2,725	2,131	2,420	1,119
1960	1,912,018	901,393	1,010,625	766,409	331,473	434,936	2,495	2,719	2,324	2,528	1,234
1961	2,016,276	981,966	1,034,310	782,510	339,047	443,463	2,576	2,896	2,331	2,612	1,236

Source: (1) *Taiwan Food Statistics Book* (1961), pp. 2-3.
      (2) *Ibid.*, p. 2.
      (3) *Ibid.*, pp. 3, 18-22.

Table 3

Sweet Potato: Production, Acreage of Plantation, and Output per Hectare, 1900-61

Year	Production (metric tons)	Acreage of Plantation (hectares)	Output per Hectare (kilograms)	Year	Production (metric tons)	Acreage of Plantation (hectares)	Output per Hectare (kilograms)
1900	205,966	39,855	5,169	1931	1,442,813	129,233	11,164
1901	238,999	53,094	4,501	1932	1,433,312	130,718	10,965
1902	300,696	61,247	4,910	1933	1,413,469	133,907	10,556
1903	538,773	71,178	7,569	1934	1,565,597	138,163	11,332
1904	681,069	90,486	7,527	1935	1,624,101	138,225	11,750
1905	684,237	98,472	6,949	1936	1,721,379	140,110	12,286
1906	682,463	94,125	7,251	1937	1,769,985	138,997	12,734
1907	725,303	105,490	6,876	1938	1,726,188	134,561	12,828
1908	880,687	118,466	7,434	1939	1,278,967	126,401	10,118
1909	786,219	106,311	7,396	1940	1,512,420	132,472	11,417
1910	642,332	102,203	6,285	1941	1,693,374	142,245	11,905
1911	677,930	104,942	6,460	1942	1,556,390	151,650	10,263
1912	673,060	110,225	6,106	1943	1,406,378	160,979	8,736
1913	822,582	116,808	7,042	1944	1,528,170	165,570	9,230
1914	821,162	113,939	7,207	1945	1,165,263	134,715	8,650
1915	809,680	110,105	7,354	1946	1,330,506	176,029	7,558
1916	717,849	107,456	6,680	1947	1,782,798	213,403	8,354
1917	734,140	107,525	6,828	1948	2,002,865	224,247	8,932
1918	815,456	115,794	7,042	1949	2,166,048	236,164	9,172
1919	998,702	119,885	8,331	1950	2,200,834	233,057	9,443
1920	836,852	112,825	7,417	1951	2,021,719	231,389	8,737
1921	892,361	120,740	7,391	1952	2,090,463	233,502	8,935
1922	949,795	120,240	7,899	1953	2,276,942	237,788	9,576
1923	986,312	121,786	8,099	1954	2,556,828	247,551	10,326
1924	1,120,301	121,110	9,250	1955	2,437,443	245,513	9,928
1925	1,145,349	122,895	9,320	1956	2,568,104	230,236	11,154
1926	1,159,109	124,515	9,309	1957	2,693,417	228,760	11,774
1927	1,275,048	124,838	10,214	1958	2,957,893	228,699	12,934
1928	1,292,882	122,817	10,527	1959	2,894,146	226,487	12,778
1929	1,180,858	123,526	9,560	1960	2,978,676	235,387	12,654
1930	1,329,902	125,180	10,624	1961	3,233,563	235,794	13,713

Sources: *Taiwan Food Statistics Book* (1961), p. 105.

Peanut: Production, Acreage of Plantation, and Output per Hectare, 1900-61

Year	Production (metric tons)	Acreage of Plantation (hectares)	Output per Hectare (kilograms)	Year	Production (metric tons)	Acreage of Plantation (hectares)	Output per Hectare (kilograms)
1900	6,103	11,598	526	1931	25,446	27,243	934
1901	5,771	12,267	470	1932	26,326	28,421	926
1902	5,501	12,939	425	1933	24,018	29,800	806
1903	8,937	15,171	589	1934	28,598	30,772	929
1904	12,067	18,991	635	1935	29,339	30,520	961
1905	10,926	19,199	569	1936	30,113	30,735	980
1906	9,485	18,391	516	1937	31,705	31,465	1,008
1907	12,196	21,028	580	1938	28,095	31,087	904
1908	13,007	21,127	616	1939	27,637	29,335	942
1909	18,952	21,427	885	1940	28,671	30,617	936
1910	9,645	19,166	503	1941	22,247	24,789	898
1911	8,686	18,149	479	1942	12,907	18,659	692
1912	8,272	18,015	459	1943	9,884	17,194	575
1913	11,109	18,831	590	1944	12,185	20,568	592
1914	9,936	19,279	515	1945	11,565	24,626	470
1915	12,083	20,447	991	1946	37,379	50,797	736
1916	11,659	20,880	558	1947	46,572	65,106	715
1917	13,827	21,593	640	1948	53,348	73,387	727
1918	16,488	23,565	700	1949	53,284	77,059	691
1919	17,870	24,714	723	1950	57,110	83,387	685
1920	14,793	22,835	648	1951	61,158	84,889	720
1921	17,482	23,647	739	1952	60,037	80,975	741
1922	18,520	23,758	780	1953	60,104	82,580	728
1923	17,792	24,253	734	1954	65,868	94,025	701
1924	20,866	25,261	826	1955	66,572	96,034	693
1925	21,618	25,296	855	1956	81,847	98,258	833
1926	22,957	26,292	873	1957	93,714	103,584	905
1927	23,748	26,334	902	1958	96,423	103,983	927
1928	23,769	26,239	906	1959	97,042	99,135	979
1929	19,393	25,676	755	1960	102,167	100,497	1,017
1930	23,497	26,712	880	1961	104,644	98,615	1,061

Sources: *Taiwan Food Statistics Book* (1961), p. 114.
Taiwan Agricultural Yearbook (1962), p. 76.

Table 5

Sugar Cane: Production, Acreage of Plantation, and Output
per Hectare, 1902-61

Year	Production (metric tons)	Acreage of Plantation (hectares)	Output per Hectare (kilograms)	Year	Production (metric tons)	Acreage of Plantation (hectares)	Output per Hectare (kilograms)
1902-03	409,894	16,029	25,572	1933-34	5,330,281	88,419	60,284
1903-04	644,985	20,944	30,796	1934-35	8,086,356	117,967	68,548
1904-05	643,334	24,225	26,557	1935-36	7,914,234	124,467	63,586
1905-06	1,014,124	34,100	29,740	1936-37	8,563,125	120,806	70,883
1906-07	833,189	29,476	28,267	1937-38	9,060,660	130,169	69,607
1907-08	851,316	27,840	30,579	1938-39	12,835,395	162,394	79,039
1908-09	1,331,683	37,860	35,174	1939-40	9,977,080	169,048	59,019
1909-10	2,160,898	61,502	35,135	1940-41	8,392,385	157,194	53,389
1910-11	2,829,153	86,753	32,612	1941-42	10,249,650	156,444	65,516
1911-12	1,895,759	73,062	25,947	1942-43	10,029,283	156,497	64,489
1912-13	819,311	65,331	14,056	1943-44	8,467,834	149,456	56,658
1913-14	1,585,570	73,981	21,432	1944-45	4,159,279	107,676	38,628
1914-15	2,360,283	82,587	28,579	1945-46	1,006,526	36,205	27,801
1915-16	3,441,131	111,006	30,999	1946-47	796,012	29,905	26,618
1916-17	5,092,870	125,759	40,497	1947-48	3,113,062	85,157	36,557
1917-18	4,090,521	145,921	28,032	1948-49	6,193,818	122,392	50,606
1918-19	3,378,803	116,786	28,932	1949-50	5,860,958	121,940	48,064
1919-20	2,629,504	105,115	25,015	1950-51	3,584,997	79,249	45,237
1920-21	2,962,994	116,280	25,482	1951-52	4,800,883	97,971	49,003
1921-22	4,051,703	137,758	29,412	1952-53	8,394,348	113,230	74,136
1922-23	3,966,578	113,111	35,067	1953-54	6,310,090	95,679	65,950
1923-24	4,676,213	119,525	39,123	1954-55	6,088,871	77,941	78,121
1924-25	5,295,505	126,553	41,844	1955-56	6,343,248	90,901	69,782
1925-26	5,169,258	119,711	44,109	1956-57	7,083,395	98,231	72,110
1926-27	4,447,178	98,475	45,160	1957-58	7,521,985	101,454	74,142
1927-28	5,818,587	105,057	55,385	1958-59	8,093,447	99,219	81,571
1928-29	7,775,167	116,433	63,343	1959-60	6,736,236	95,543	70,505
1929-30	6,971,015	106,104	65,700	1960-61	7,922,383	100,180	79,082
1930-31	6,566,802	96,111	68,325				
1931-32	8,049,285	106,215	75,783				
1932-33	5,286,720	81,792	64,636				

Sources: *Economic History of Taiwan Under the Japanese Control* (in Chinese), I, pp. 41-42.
Taiwan Agricultural Yearbook (1962), p. 5.

134

Table 6

General Price Index, 1910-61
(1935-37 = 100)

Year	Price Index	Year	Price Index	Year	Price Index
1910	50.15	1928	103.24	1945	2,721.21
1911	52.02	1929	100.18	1946	10,813.19
1912	60.28	1930	89.33	1947	52,062.42
1913	61.47	1931	80.26	1948	433,251.05
1914	58.93	1932	81.91	1949	748.39
1915	62.29	1933	87.63	1950	1,009.39
1916	72.95	1934	91.22	1951	1,673.43
1917	89.81	1935	92.81	1952	2,062.89
1918	115.38	1936	95.99	1953	2,243.66
1919	131.17	1937	111.20	1954	2,296.77
1920	151.68	1938	132.58	1955	2,620.33
1921	117.74	1939	152.25	1956	2,953.25
1922	118.03	1940	172.03	1957	3,166.55
1923	113.85	1941	187.15	1958	3,210.62
1924	115.38	1942	184.99	1959	3,633.97
1925	114.97	1943	315.97	1960	4,148.13
1926	109.37	1944	529.96	1961	4,282.21
1927	106.60				

Source: JCRR data.

Table 7

Index on Farm Rice Price, 1901–40 and 1949–60
(1938 = 100) (1957 = 100)

Year	Price Index	Year	Price Index	Year	Price Index	Year	Price Index
	(1938 = 100)						(1957 = 100)
1901	23.5	1919	110.8	1936	92.4	1949	17.4
1902	29.6	1920	92.9	1937	93.3	1950	29.8
1903	34.1	1921	73.1	1938	100.0	1951	34.3
1904	23.7	1922	61.1	1939	109.0	1952	63.1
1905	27.4	1923	72.7	1940	111.5	1953	94.2
1906	33.4	1924	88.8			1954	70.3
1907	45.3	1925	104.0			1955	91.1
1908	33.9	1926	95.7			1956	90.3
1909	30.5	1927	78.2			1957	100.0
1910	35.1	1928	81.4			1958	101.2
1911	46.7	1929	81.4			1959	109.5
1912	57.8	1930	60.0			1960	165.9
1913	52.6	1931	47.0				
1914	39.7	1932	85.3				
1915	32.1	1933	61.9				
1916	37.8	1934	75.0				
1917	55.3	1935	89.3				
1918	83.1						

Source: E. L. Rada and T. H. Lee, *Irrigation Investment in Taiwan* (Taipei: JCRR, 1963), pp. 139–41.

Table 8

Index on Price Ratio Between Agricultural and All Commodities, 1911-60
(1935-37 = 100)

Year	Price Ratio	Year	Price Ratio	Year	Price Ratio
1911	114.89	1928	101.88	1945	18.85
1912	113.22	1929	105.58	1946	150.59
1913	107.04	1930	95.38	1947	125.89
1914	95.04	1931	84.87	1948	87.94
1915	79.10	1932	112.61	1949	62.46
1916	72.57	1933	84.97	1950	73.21
1917	76.97	1934	91.99	1951	62.16
1918	84.69	1935	104.22	1952	66.93
1919	95.72	1936	104.39	1953	81.34
1920	79.87	1937	92.69	1954	65.44
1921	93.33	1938	84.91	1955	74.21
1922	74.21	1939	88.09	1956	67.71
1923	81.17	1940	87.74	1957	69.39
1924	89.86	1941	86.29	1958	70.47
1925	103.57	1942	94.97	1959	71.04
1926	105.23	1943	55.84	1960	81.80
1927	96.91	1944	46.93		

Source: Calculations based on data in Appendix Tables 1 and 6.

Table 9

Total and Agricultural Population, 1905-61
(Unit: 1,000 persons)

| Year | Total | Agricultural | Percentage of Agricultural Population to Total Population | Year | Total | Agricultural | Percentage of Agricultural Population to Total Population |
	(1)	(2)	(2)/(1) x 100 (3)		(1)	(2)	(2)/(1) x 100 (3)
1905	3,123	1,962	62.80	1951	7,869	4,161	52.87
1910	3,299	2,087	63.25	1952	8,128	4,257	52.37
1915	3,570	2,280	63.86	1953	8,428	4,382	51.93
1920	3,758	2,227	59.25	1954	8,749	4,489	51.30
1925	4,147	2,340	56.41	1955	9,078	4,603	50.71
1930	4,679	2,534	54.16	1956	9,390	4,699	50.04
1935	5,316	2,790	54.29	1957	9,690	4,790	49.43
1940	6,077	2,984	49.10	1958	10,039	4,881	48.62
1945	...	3,366	...	1959	10,431	4,975	47.69
1949	7,397	3,879	52.44	1960	10,792	5,373	49.79
1950	7,555	3,998	52.93	1961	11,149	...	...

Source: Data before 1950 were from *Taiwan Agricultural Statistics 1901-1955* (Taipei: JCRR, Dec., 1956), p. 7. Data for and after 1949 were from *Taiwan Statistical Data Book* (1962).

Table 10

Labor Force: Total Agricultural and Nonagricultural, 1905-61
(Unit: 1,000 persons)

Year	Total Labor Force	Agricultural		Nonagricultural	
		Number	Percentage of Total	Number	Percentage of Total
1905	1,404	993	71	417	29
1915	1,643	1,165	71	478	29
1920	1,637	1,137	69	500	31
1930	1,790	1,212	68	578	32
1940	2,244	1,400	62	844	38
1949	2,828	1,773	62.7	1,055	37.3
1950	2,849	1,788	62.8	1,061	37.2
1951	2,881	1,785	62.0	1,096	38.0
1952	2,936	1,792	61.0	1,144	39.0
1953	2,954	1,812	61.3	1,142	38.7
1954	3,000	1,811	60.4	1,189	39.6
1955	3,026	1,812	59.9	1,214	40.1
1956	3,015	1,806	59.9	1,209	40.1
1957	3,110	1,810	58.2	1,300	41.8
1958	3,178	1,813	57.0	1,365	43.0
1959	3,272	1,853	56.6	1,419	43.4
1960	3,344	1,877	56.1	1,467	43.9
1961	3,429	1,912	55.8	1,517	44.2

Source: Data preceding 1950 from B. Johnson, "Agricultural Development and Economic Transformation: A Comparative Study of Japanese Experience,"(Food Research Institute Studies, Vol. III, Nov., 1962), p. 266. Data for and after 1949, *Taiwan Statistical Data Book* (1962).

Table 11

Balance of Payments of Taiwan, 1896-1944

(Unit: T$1000)

Year	(1) Exports F.O.B.	(2) Imports C.I.F.	(3) Trade Balance	(4) Shipping	(5) Government Transfers (+) in (-) out	(6) Other Transfers (+) in (-) out	(7) Currency, Gold & Silver Bars (net)	(8) Accomm. Capital Movements & Errors & Omissions	(9) Cumulative of (8)
1896	11,396	8,631	+ 2,765	n.a.	+ 6,940	n.a.	- 3,337	- 6,368	- 6,368
1897	14,857	16,383	- 1,526	n.a.	+ 5,959	n.a.	- 3,564	- 869	- 7,237
1898	16,963	21,142	- 4,180	- 189	+ 3,984	n.a.	- 7,904	+ 8,289	+ 1,052
1899	14,743	22,285	- 7,542	- 198	+ 3,000	n.a.	- 1,278	+ 6,018	+ 7,070
1900	14,934	22,010	- 7,075	- 210	+ 2,598	+ 7,945	+ 2,499	+ 5,707	+ 1,363
1901	15,580	21,592	- 6,012	- 239	+ 2,386	+ 6,072	- 306	- 1,901	- 538
1902	21,132	19,336	+ 1,796	- 196	+ 2,459	- 1,020	- 3,016	+ 23	- 561
1903	20,716	22,204	- 1,488	- 201	+ 2,459	- 2,123	- 2,646	+ 3,999	+ 3,458
1904	22,719	22,746	- 28	- 167	+ 700	- 1,700	+ 893	+ 302	+ 3,740
1905	24,291	24,448	- 157	- 189	....	+ 2,844	+ 360	+ 2,138	+ 1,602
1906	28,039	28,372	- 333	- 221	....	+ 389	+ 3,431	+ 2,490	- 888
1907	27,376	30,971	- 3,595	- 210	....	+ 6,175	+ 517	+ 2,887	- 3,775
1908	33,721	38,002	- 4,280	- 221	....	+ 6,116	- 1,656	+ 41	- 3,734
1909	47,997	36,598	+ 11,399	- 245	....	- 18,971	+ 880	+ 6,937	+ 3,203
1910	59,962	48,923	+ 11,039	- 190	....	+ 6,843	+ 663	+ 3,343	- 140
1911	64,819	53,295	+ 11,525	- 366	....	+ 8,292	+ 193	+ 3,060	- 3,200
1912	62,792	62,632	+ 159	- 432	....	+ 9,510	+ 292	+ 8,945	- 12,145
1913	53,389	60,859	- 7,470	- 468	....	+ 9,013	+ 162	+ 913	- 13,058
1914	58,720	52,913	+ 5,808	- 441	....	+ 5,905	+ 760	- 12,032	- 25,090
1915	75,623	53,410	+ 22,214	- 458	....	- 35,491	+ 1,786	+ 11,949	- 13,141
1916	112,348	65,922	+ 47,326	- 557	....	- 57,584	+ 1,325	+ 9,490	- 3,651
1917	145,804	88,887	+ 56,916	- 639	....	- 44,970	+ 28	- 11,279	- 14,930
1918	139,356	104,219	+ 35,137	- 761	....	- 15,050	- 1,844	- 17,482	- 32,412
1919	177,831	154,705	+ 23,125	- 760	....	+ 32,500	- 2,060	- 52,805	- 85,217

140

Year	(1)	(2)	(3)	(4)	(5)	(6)	(7)	(8)
1920	216,205	172,437	+ 43,827	- 1,011	...	+ 26,202	- 2,138	- 152,097
1921	152,439	133,954	+ 18,484	- 1,196	...	+ 29,400	- 603	- 198,182
1922	157,865	119,095	+ 38,770	- 1,076	...	+ 6,113	- 2,129	- 239,860
1923	198,595	110,129	+ 88,465	- 1,063	...	- 19,767	- 2,484	- 305,011
1924	253,674	133,026	+120,648	- 1,090	...	- 41,157	- 2,330	- 381,082
1925	263,215	186,395	+ 76,819	- 1,118	...	- 1,692	- 3,146	- 451,945
1926	251,425	183,412	+ 68,013	- 1,226	...	- 22,642	- 2,608	- 493,482
1927	246,676	186,948	+ 59,728	- 1,235	...	- 42,136	- 978	- 508,861
1928	248,417	190,654	+ 57,763	- 1,301	...	+ 17,378	- 2,539	- 580,162
1929	271,893	204,911	+ 66,983	- 1,434	...	- 41,866	- 2,089	- 601,756
1930	241,441	168,258	+ 73,183	- 1,388	...	- 24,154	- 3,763	- 645,634
1931	220,673	145,622	+ 75,251	- 1,287	...	- 13,360	- 3,191	- 703,047
1932	240,728	164,498	+ 76,230	- 1,314	...	- 36,499	- 2,412	- 739,052
1933	248,413	165,389	+ 63,024	- 1,413	...	- 20,292	- 2,525	- 777,846
1934	305,929	215,022	+ 90,907	- 1,434	...	- 42,150	- 3,077	- 822,092
1935	350,745	263,110	+ 87,625	- 1,729	...	- 14,765	+12,673	- 905,896
1936	387,949	292,686	+ 95,263	- 1,831	...	- 31,525	- 4,031	- 963,772
1937	440,175	322,124	+118,051	- 1,823	- 116,836	+122,998	...	...
1938	456,454	366,659	+ 89,795	- 1,973	- 13,236	+109,346	...	...
1939	592,938	408,650	+184,288	- 2,590	- 88,586	- 37,151	...	...
1940	566,054	481,813	+ 84,242	- 3,024	- 104,695	...	...	...
1941	493,904	424,507	+ 69,396	- 3,172	- 125,000	...	...	...
1942	523,139	384,519	+138,620	- 1,809	- 175,500	...	...	...
1943	400,903	338,727	+ 62,176	n.a.	- 232,500	...	...	...
1944	311,204	164,722	+146,432	n.a.	- 275,000	...	...	...

Sources: (a) Columns (1), (2) and (3) *Statistical Abstract of Taiwan Province During the Fifty-one-Year Period* (in Chinese) (Taipei, 1946), p. 918.

(b) Column (4) *ibid.*, pp. 1202-3 (Only outgoing passenger fares: for years before 1910, we take one half of total passenger fares because the data do not give breakdown between outgoing and incoming fares.)

(c) Column (5) T. Wang, C. H. Chang and C. C. Li, *Taiwan's Public Finance During the Period Under the Japanese Control* (in Chinese) (Taipei: JCRR, 1951), pp. 20 and 85.

(d) Column (6) Figures for Years 1900-1920: *Financial Affairs of Taiwan Reference Book*, various years (in Chinese) (Derived from the total foreign exchange receipts and payments with adjustment made for net trade balance and shipping service.) Figures for 1921-39: *Commercial & Industrial Statistics of Taiwan* (in Chinese) (various years).

(e) Column (7) *Statistical Abstract of Taiwan Province During the Fifty-one Year Period* (in Chinese) (Taipei, 1946), Table 920.

(f) Column (8) Sum of Columns (3), (4), (5), (6), and (7) and reverse the sign.

Table 12

Japanese Immigration to Taiwan (Net), 1897-1942
(Unit: Number of persons)

Year	Agriculture & Fishery	Mining & Industries	Commerce & Communication	Civil Service & Professional	Others
1897	2,041	3,601	11,990	3,821	7,127
1898	158	1,681	3,681	...	4,616
1899	282	858	4,568	3,793	3,339
1900	1,123	643	3,720	1,403	2,815
1901	763	- 30	667	1,185	1,125
1902	366	- 137	256	382	1,502
1903	481	110	511	3	1,327
1904	519	- 100	62	30	-1,261
1905	477	79	816	221	1,058
1906	245	292	- 2,092	196	3,187
1907	726	537	8	786	1,730
1908	844	235	813	706	3,468
1909	880	300	628	558	1,951
1910	1,448	783	2,509	1,262	6,905
1911	1,832	564	749	1,604	6,528
1912	3,225	69	1,298	1,118	8,128
1913	2,570	340	493	1,398	6,557
1914	1,090	- 141	2,033	2,899	3,051
1915	1,995	4	2,351	381	6,380
1916	3,004	39	- 360	788	5,365
1917	744	- 336	- 574	519	6,980
1918	1,021	186	955	944	3,347
1919	988	366	546	1,429	6,385
1920	1,039	841	1,887	1,999	6,932
1921	152	343	1,972	1,231	6,363
1922	469	- 331	- 630	2,411	4,902
1923	522	223	890	- 485	3,077
1924	752	315	836	2,287	1,578
1925	- 416	234	2,278	3,093	4,220
1926	- 167	197	1,489	2,386	2,671
1927	167	379	4,288	2,735	7,830
1928	620	174	15	889	2,818
1929	938	375	2,141	287	1,906
1930	2,074	356	2,925	1,747	1,537
1931	- 340	168	1,350	1,073	1,509
1932	- 386	41	3,047	1,108	2,128
1933	248	132	4,268	166	-2,887
1934	757	155	4,452	330	-2,499
1935	1,059	- 89	1,414	1,002	72
1936	1,294	761	2,419	2,903	-1,260
1937	1,808	802	593	2,240	3,996
1938	3,339	2,527	661	6,123	1,919
1939	2,120	1,248	2,589	6,861	27,050
1940	1,493	1,563	3,597	7,885	8,715
1941	1,393	3,819	6,192	957	9,936
1942	78	- 142	611	3,781	8,333

Source: *Statistical Abstract of Taiwan Province During the Fifty-one Year Period* (in Chinese) (Taipei, 1946), Table 95.

NOTES

NOTES

CHAPTER 1

1. Economic Survey of Asia and the Far East, 1964 (New York: United Nations, 1965), p. 8.

2. Gustav F. Papanek, "Development Problems Relevant to Agricultural Tax Policy," Papers and Proceedings of the Conference on Agricultural Taxation and Economic Development (Cambridge: Harvard University Printing Office, 1954).

3. Philip M. Raup, "Agricultural Taxation and Land Tenure Reform in Underdeveloped Countries," Papers and Proceedings of the Conference on Agricultural Taxation and Economic Development (Cambridge: Harvard University Printing Office, 1954), pp. 246-55; N. S. Buchanan and H. S. Ellis, Approaches to Economic Development (New York: The Twentieth Century Fund, 1955), pp. 243-49; W. A. Lewis, The Theory of Economic Growth (Homewood, Ill.: Richard D. Irwin, 1955), pp. 120-27; A. Pepelasis, L. Mears, and I. Adelman, Economic Development (New York: Harper and Brothers, 1961), pp. 30-37.

4. Warriner complained that economists have neglected the subject because they accept the existing institution as given and said, "This neglect is unfortunate, because it means we have no accepted method of analysis, and lack even proper terminology." Doreen Warriner, Land Reform and Economic Development, p. 3, reprinted in C. K. Eicher and Lawrence W. Witt, Agriculture in Economic Development (New York: McGraw-Hill, 1964), pp. 11-44. Her point may be applicable to the more recent writers but certainly not to the classical ones. From the time of Adam Smith's chapter "Of the Rent of Land," in Book I of The Wealth of Nations, through John Stuart Mill's chapters "On Peasant Proprietors" (VI), "Of Metayers" (VIII), and "Of Cottiers" (IX), in his Principles of Political Economy to Alfred Marshall's analysis in Chapter 10, Book VI of the Principles, economists have paid much attention to the role of the system of land tenure.

5. A. (Burk) Berguson, "A Reformulation of Certain Aspects of Welfare Economics," Quarterly Journal of Economics LII (February, 1938), reprinted in his Essays in Normative Economics Cambridge: Harvard University Press, 1966), pp. 3-26.

6. For a more detailed description of the natural conditions of Taiwan, see Chiao-min Hsieh, Taiwan-ilha formosa: A Geography in Perspective (London: Butterworths, 1964).

7. Demographic Year Book (United Nations, 1960).

8. The study is based on statistical data up to 1960, although figures for some tables are carried to 1961 and 1962. The choice of the cut-off date is intentional because by 1960, we believe that the immediate impact of the land reform should have been fully eliminated.

CHAPTER 2

1. See Appendix Table 1.

2. For the story of administrative leadership of these programs, see Chang Han-Yu and R. H. Myers, "Japanese Colonial Development Policy in Taiwan, 1895-1906 — A case of Bureaucratic Entrepreneurship," Journal of Asian Studies, XVII (August, 1963), pp. 433-49.

3. Economic History of Taiwan (in Chinese), 7 (Taipei: Bureau of Economic Research, Bank of Taiwan, 1959).

4. To get an idea of price movements in the early years, we rely on the index of farm price for rice. It was 23 in 1901 (1938 = 100) and 111 in 1919. A change of such magnitude within eighteen years cannot be considered stable. Using the aggregate agricultural index (1935-37 = 100), we find a doubling of the price between 1912 and 1919. In the depression years of the 1930's, the price dropped to one half of the 1919 level; in the war years of the early 1940's the price index skyrocketed to 513 by 1945 (see Appendix Table 7).

5. Economic History of Taiwan (in Chinese),1 (Taipei: Bureau of Economic Research, Bank of Taiwan, 1958), pp. 6-7.

6. Statistical Abstract of Taiwan Province During the Fifty-one-Year Period (in Chinese) (Taipei, 1946), Table 213 (Benefits from the Conservancy Projects on Rivers).

7. Ibid., Table 212 (Damage and Loss from the Flooding of Rivers).

8. Improvement of rice varieties has always made important changes in land utilization and production in China. The introduction in the eleventh century of early ripening and relatively drought-resistant rice from Champa (a state in central Indochina) to Fukien ensured the success of the double-cropping system. Moreover, the early ripening rice, which requires much less water than the other varieties, made possible the cultivation of higher land and hilly slopes. See Ping-ti Ho, Studies on the Population of China 1368-1953 (Cambridge: Harvard University Press, 1959), pp. 169-76.

9. In terms of index, it was 38.5 in 1901–10 and 100 in 1938. Source: Taiwan Agricultural Yearbook and Taiwan Food Statistics Book, various years.

10. The following table shows a dramatic contrast of response to fertilizer application. Even at the level of fertilizer treatment considered normal for Chailai, Ponlai response exceeded Chailai by as much as 18 per cent. When fertilizers were applied at levels beyond normal, the difference became even greater and when twice as much fertilizers as the normal (at level 4 in the table) were used, Ponlai rice reached a productivity index of 182 which was 50 per cent higher than the highest output for Chailai rice at its normal level of fertilizer treatment (112).

Application of Fertilizer and Rice Productivity

Experiment specification	Index	
	Ponlai Rice	Chailai Rice
Level 0 (no fertilizer)	100	100
Level 1 (50 per cent less fertilizer than normal level)	111	110
Level 2 (normal)	130	112
Level 3 (50 per cent more fertilizer than normal level)	156	108
Level 4 (100 per cent more fertilizer than normal level)	182	106

Source: Data from the Central Agricultural Experimental Station, 1924, as quoted in Economic History of Taiwan (in Chinese), 7 (Taipei: Bureau of Economic Research, Bank of Taiwan, 1958), p. 46.

11. See Chang and Myers, op. cit., pp. 562–63, for a history of the use of local and regional agricultural associations as agents of dissemination of technology and production methods.

12. In some cases, local police compelled the farmers to switch from other crops to the growth of sugar cane, as reported in R. H.

Myers and A. Ching, "Agricultural Development in Taiwan Under Japanese Control," Journal of Asian Studies, XXIII (August, 1964), p. 565 and ftn. 10, pp. 559-60.

13. For an interesting graphic representation of a combined impact of different sugar-cane species and the percentage of sugar-cane field devoted to each on the average yield of sugar cane in Taiwan, see Taiwan's Sugar (in Chinese), (Taipei: Bureau of Economic Research, Bank of Taiwan, 1949), pp. 4-5.

14.

Net Receipt per Hectare
(Unit: Taiwan dollars)

	Sugar Cane (1926-27)		Paddy Rice (1926)		
	Paddy Field	Dry Land	First Crop	Second Crop	Total
Owner-cultivator	118.98	107.17	88.78	36.34	125.12
Tenant	98.14	117.41	60.27	42.25	102.52

Source: A Study of Relative Price Between Rice and Sugar in Taiwan (in Chinese) (Taipei: Bureau of Economic Research, Bank of Taiwan, 1933), pp. 44 and 56-57.

15. There are variants to the scheme. For the Imperial Sugar-Manufacturing Company, the price of sugar cane was set by contract with sugar-cane producers about a year and a half ahead. At the time of harvest, the preset price was considered the base price to be adjusted by a sliding scale formula based on the then prevailing price of rice. The formula varied from year to year.

The Taiwan Sugar-Manufacturing Company used a sliding scale formula based on the date of planting the sugar-cane seedling by the farmers. The earlier in the season of planting, the larger was the subsidy (Taiwan Sugar Yearbook, various years). Under both schemes, the subsidy was greater for sugar cane grown on two-crop paddy fields than on one-crop paddy fields, which was in turn higher than for those grown on dry land. Taiwan Sugar Yearbook (various years), as quoted in Economic History of Taiwan, 4 (Taipei: Bureau of Economic Research, Bank of Taiwan, 1956, p. 81.

16. When the sugar-cane buying price in Central Taiwan was regressed against the prices of sugar and rice for the period 1917-29,

we find that the regression coefficient for the sugar price was statistically insignificant, while that for the rice price significant.*

X_1 = price of sugar (T$ per 100 kilograms)

X_2 = price of rice (T$ per 100 kilograms)

x_3 = price of sugar cane in Taichung (T$ per 1000 kilograms)

X_4 = price of sugar cane in Changhwa (T$ per 1000 kilograms)

X_3 = 3.0103 + 0.0647 X_1 + 0.3201 X_2 R = 0.9185

    (2.2334) (0.0440) (0.1637) (DF corrected)

X_4 = -0.0645 + 0.0330 X_1 + 0.6307 X_2 R = 0.9185

    (1.2799) + (0.0252) + (0.0938) (DF corrected)

* Taichung prices were set by the Imperial Sugar-Manufacturing Company, while the Changhwa prices were set by the Hsinkao Sugar-Manufacturing Company.

Source: A Study of Relative Price, p. 51.

17.

Percentage Distribution of Sugar-Manufacturing Costs, 1909-44
(Unit: Percentage)

Year	Raw Material	Manufacturing	Administrative
1909-18	56.74	13.67	29.59
1919-28	63.32	11.70	24.98
1929-38	58.37	13.89	27.74
1939-44 (5 years)	52.58	15.75	31.67

Source: A Study of Relative Price, pp. 70-71.

18.

Relative Price Between Sugar and Rice in Taiwan, 1914-43
(in terms of rice price)

Year	Excluding Sugar Consumption Tax	Including Sugar Consumption Tax
1914-28	2.80	0.75
1924-33	1.76	1.01
1934-43	1.69	1.00

Source: A Study of Relative Price, pp. 54-55.

19.　　　Yield per Hectare of Sugar Cane, 1908-44
(in terms of kilograms of rice productivity)*

Year	Relative Yield
1909-14 (5 years)	0.6377
1915-24	0.7077
1925-34	1.4833
1935-44	1.5066

* Based on yield of three crops of rice.
Source: ibid., p. 35.

20. See Charles P. Kindleberger, The Terms of Trade: A European Case Study (MIT Press and Wiley and Sons, 1956), p. 306. "Luck may find a country with fixed resources engaged in the production of commodities which are in good demand (Belgian iron and steel, Swedish timber) or in bad demand (Italian marble, French wine), but flexibility provides a guarantee of reasonable terms of trade."

21. Surprisingly enough, the Japanese authorities also included under this heading expenses for implementing the expansion into Southern China and the southeast Pacific. This item was stricken from the above headings, not so much because of the way the money was intended or used, as for its incompatibility with all other items under the same heading. Indeed a large part of the money was classified as "foreign travel"; other funds were either for salary or dealing with "matters of confidence."

22. Ibid., p. 325. In Economic History of Taiwan, the percentage figures do not add to 100 because of rounding and omission of miscellaneous tax receipts.

23.　　　Public and Private Investment, 1896-1944
(Unit: $1,000 in 1935-37 Taiwan dollars)

Year	(1) Public Investment and Subsidies	(2) Private Investment	(3) Sum	(4) [(2) as percentage of (3)]
1896-1905	104,458	5,794	110,252	5
1906-15	176,070	146,531	322,601	45
1916-25	146,228	272,670	418,898	65
1926-35	245,626	92,119	337,745	27
1936-44	309,377	561,051	870,428	64
		1,078,165	2,059,924	52

Source: Statistical Abstract, Tables 304, 335, and 366.

24. For details of construction, see footnotes to the Balance of Payments of Taiwan (Appendix Table 11).

25. Andrew J. Grajdanzer, Formosa Today (New York: Institute of Pacific Relations, 1942), p. 147.

26. Financial Subsidy by Japan and Government Receipts
in Taiwan, 1896-1904

Year	Percentage
1896	72.0
1897	53.0
1898	34.0
1899	17.2
1900	11.7
1901	12.1
1902	12.6
1903	12.3
1904	3.1

Source: Taiwan's Public Finance During the Period Under the Japanese Control (in Chinese) (Taipei: JCRR), p. 20.

27. No data are found on government transfers or other autonomous foreign capital movement to Taiwan during the period 1905-30.

28. We have no way to estimate the amount of capital that might have been brought to Taiwan, in terms of personal belongings, by Japanese immigrants.

CHAPTER 3

1. Quoted in Ping-ti Ho, Studies on the Population of China 1368-1953 (Cambridge: Harvard University Press, 1959), p. 219.

2. Statistical Abstract of Taiwan Province During the Fifty-one Year Period (in Chinese) (Taipei, 1946), Tables 49 and 196.

3. Ibid., Table 194.

4. Ibid., Table 198.

5. In 1961, the prices and value of rice output were more than 5 times the value of the next important common crop, sweet potatoes, and 7 times the value of sugar cane. Taiwan Agricultural Yearbook (1962), p. 32.

6. Taichung 31 and Taichung 32 are two varieties of wheat. The former was derived by crossing Saitama, an early Japanese variety of spring wheat and Showa Wase, another Japanese variety; the latter by

crossing Saitama with Florence. T. H. Shen, Agricultural Development on Taiwan Since World War II (Ithaca, N.Y.: Comstock Publishing Associates, 1964), p. 203.

7. Shen, ibid., p. 156.

8. The figures were compiled by Taiwan Provincial Land Bureau, 1949, as quoted in H. S. Tang's Land Reform in Free China (Taipei: JCRR, 1954), p. 46.

9. Ministry of Interior, June, 1951, quoted in C. Cheng, Land Reform in Taiwan (Taipei: China Publishing Co., 1961), p. 45.

10. Findings of the Cabinet Rent Reduction Inspection Team, op. cit.

11. Tang, op. cit., p. 63.

12.

Number of Tenant Families Purchasing Land
and the Area Purchased 1949-53

	1949	1950	1951	1952	1953	Total
1. Number of tenant families	1,722	6,989	11,018	17,639	28,960	66,328
2. Area (chia)	773	3,356	5,885	9,862	15,646	35,522
3. (1) as per cent of those who signed the 37.5% lease contract.	0.6	2.4	3.7	5.8	...	...
4. (2) as per cent of the total area of farmland regulated by the 37.5% lease contract.	0.3	1.3	2.2	3.8	...	...

Source: Statistics in the enforcement of the 37.5 per cent limitation program compiled by the Taiwan Provincial Land Bureau, quoted in Tang, op. cit., pp. 64-65.

13. C. Cheng op. cit., p. 311. The apparent difference in figures quoted above from those of Tang's in Land Reform in Free China is due to the fact that Cheng's figures included the sales of public lands in 1958.

14. Progress Report on the Land-to-the-Tiller Program (The Taiwan Land Bank).

15. Cheng, op. cit., p. 312.

16. H. S. Tang and S. C. Hsieh, "Land Reform and Agricultural Development in Taiwan," in Walter Froehlich (ed.), Land Tenure Industrialization and Social Stability (Milwaukee: Marquette University Press, 1961), p. 125.

17. The 1921 data are in units of chia (Statistical Abstract), whereas the 1950-52 data of Tang and Hsieh, op. cit., were collected by hectare. Since there is no way to rearrange the data into class intervals with the same unit of measure, the statement made in the text should be qualified by a margin of error to the extent that 1.0 chia = 0.9699 hectare.

18.
Average Size of Farms and Farm Families 1900-60

Period	Farm Families (numbers)	Area (hectares)	Average Size of Farms (hectares)	Average Size of Farm Families (persons)
1900-1909	368,787	554,481	1.50	5.52
1910-19	373,164	704,248	1.89	5.95
1920-29	395,715	774,110	1.96	5.40
1930-39	417,685	833,369	2.00	6.56
1940-49	507,472	843,944	1.66	6.69
1950-59	718,628	875,070	1.22	6.29
1960	785,592	869,223	1.11	6.84

Source: E. L. Rada and T. H. Lee, Irrigation Investment in Taiwan (Taipei: JCRR, 1963), p. 18.

19. Redemarcation of Land in Taiwan (Department of Information, Taiwan Provincial Government, March, 1962); and Development of Taiwan, 1945-1962 (in Chinese) (Department of Information, Taiwan Provincial Government, 1962), Chapter 6, Section 2.

20. A ten-year redemarcation program for the farmland has been worked out for a total of 300,000 hectares, starting in 1962. The first year saw 4,527 hectares redemarcated with an average cost of NT$3,500 per hectare, which compares favorably with the per hectare cost of NT$4,660 in 1961 and shows a saving of NT$1,160.

CHAPTER 4

1. See Table 20.

2. Assuming that the rent before reduction was 50 per cent of the main crop plus some fringe benefits accrued to the landlords, a rent limitation to 37.5 per cent of the main crop and the removal of the privilege of landlords to impose other assessment on the tenants could amount to a lowering of the net return to the landlords by as much as 30 per cent below the original. A 30 per cent reduction of the original valuation (or 3.5 times the annual yield) gives approximately the figure of 2.5 times of annual yield.

3.

Value of Government Stocks Paid to Landlords as 30 per cent of the Compensation for Land Compulsorily Purchased in June, 1954

Corporation	Value of Government Stocks (NT$)	Value of Government Stocks Paid to Landlords (NT$)	Percentage of Total Value of Stock
Taiwan Cement Corporation	247,148,280	243,647,610	37
Taiwan Paper and Pulp Corporation	219,966,000	217,250,150	33
Taiwan Agricultural and Forestry Developmnet Corporation	138,821,590	86,359,540	13
Taiwan Industrial and Mining Corporation	184,088,300	112,517,340	17
Total	790,024,170	659,774,640	100

Source: H. S. Tang, Land Reform in Free China (Taipei: JCRR, 1954), p. 168.

4.
Classification of Landlords Interviewed

(1)	(2)	(3)	(4)	(5)
Classification of Landlord	Number Investi- gated	Average Area of Land Originally Owned (hectares)	Average Area of Land Compulsorily Purchased (hectares)	(4)/(3) Percentage
Small holders (less than 10 ha.)	13	5.92	4.11	69.43
Medium holders (10-50 ha.)	7	27.60	22.01	79.75
Large holders (more than 50 ha.)	4	174.56	139.58	79.08
All holders	24	40.35	31.91	79.08

Source: H. S. Tang and S. C. Hsieh, "Land Reform and Agricultural Development in Taiwan," in Walter Froehlich (ed.), Land Tenure Industrialization and Social Stability (Milwaukee: Marquette University Press, 1961).

5.
Sale of Land Bonds and Industrial Stocks by Landlords
(Unit: Number of landlords)

Landlord	Land Bond	Taiwan Cement	Taiwan Paper and Pulp	Taiwan Agricultural and Forestry	Taiwan Industrial and Mining
Small holders	3	9	10	10	10
Medium holders	1	5	5	5	5
Large holders	...	1	4	3	4

Source: Tang and Hsieh, ibid.

6. There were 9,000 individual and 104 institutional stockholders in March, 1961. A frequency distribution table of the stockholders was first made. Then we proceeded to determine the number of shares of the Cement Corporation stock paid to landlords in addition to bonds and other stocks for each hectare of land compulsorily purchased. Altogether, 121,535 hectares of paddy and 22,033 hectares of dry land were compulsorily purchased; in terms of average value (December, 1952), the dry land is less than 8 per cent that of paddy. Thus, we concentrate our analysis on the landlords of paddy fields. Out of their total compensation (388,722 metric tons of paddy rice), 30 per cent was paid in industrial stocks. On a per hectare basis, it was 3.15737 metric tons worth of paddy rice or NT$5051.792 (based on December, 1952, price of NT$1600 per metric tons) in industrial stocks, of which 37 per cent was paid in the Cement Corporation stock. Since the par value was NT$10 per share, we get 186.92 shares of the Cement stock for each hectare of paddy field.

Estimated Number of Cement Corporation Stocks
Distributed to Ex-Landlords

Class Interval	(1)* Paddy Fields Sold (hectares)	(2)** Number of Cement Stocks Distributed (shares)	(3) Largest Individual Stock-holders (shares)	(4)*** Number of Shares According to Stock-holders' List (shares)	(5) (4)/(2) Percent-age
Less than 0.5 ha.	11,582	2,164,907	93	98,364	4.5
0.5-less than 1.0 ha.	19,142	3,578,123	187	164,565	4.6
1.0-less than 1.5 ha.	15,495	2,896,325	280	163,576	5.6
1.5-less than 2.0 ha.	11,534	2,155,935	374	148,261	6.8
2.0-less than 3.0 ha.	15,520	2,900,998	561	272,733	9.3
3.0-and higher	48,298	9,027,862			
	121,535	22,724,150			

Source: * Table 12.
   ** Tang, op. cit., p. 149.
  *** Stockholders' List of the Cement Corporation March, 1961).

In the table above, we use the figures in Column 3 to calculate the maximum number of Cement Corporation stocks that an individual landlord could get within each interval and then check the stockholders list and count the number of shares of the Cement Corporation stock that was held by the stockholders of a certain size (i.e., those who held less than 100 shares, and 101-200 shares, etc.). As an example, in the class interval of less than 0.5 hectares in the table, 11,582 hectares were sold with each less than 0.5 hectares. The total number of the Cement Corporation shares paid to landlords became 2,164,907 shares (Column 2 derived by 186.92 x 11,582) and no landlord received more than 93 shares, because 0.5 hectare is the limit of the class interval (Column 3). Similarly, we derive the total number of shares distributed to the landlords of each class interval. From the frequency table of the Cement Corporation stockholders, we know 98,364 shares were held by stockholders who owned 100 or less (Column 4), and 164,565 by stockholders who owned between 100 and 200 shares, etc. By comparing the number of shares that were originally distributed within each size category of land sold by the landlords (Column 2) with those held as of 1961 (Column 4) and expressing the latter as per cent of the former, we trace out the percentage of retention of the Cement Corporation stocks according to the size of landholdings. One important qualification of the estimate, among others, is that about 8 per cent of the Cement Corporation stocks was always held by private investors and they were not subject to distribution by the government to the landlords.

    7. Food Production and Activities of the Taiwan Provincial Food Bureau (Taipei), p. 41.

    8. See Chapter 6 for a discussion of the economic implications of the fertilizer-rice barter ratio.

    9. Similar calculations are made, based on the average yield of paddy rice and brown rice. The calculations are omitted and the average productivity figures are shown in Appendix Table 2, for both brown and paddy rice. The consequence of each of these three sets of figures upon the estimated increase of income needs a comment. The higher productivity figure used by the Land Bureau or the Food Bureau, as compared with the lower average figures, results in a higher income in absolute terms. In terms of percentage change, the initial higher production figure means a lower growth rate. In Table 13 there is an increment in income from 1948 by 1,957 kilograms of rice, while in similar calculations, using the lower yield figures of paddy and brown rice, we have increments of 1,337 kilograms and 1,656 kilograms, respectively, from 1948. The rate of growth from 1949 as the base year is 340 per cent for Table 13, 350 per cent and 289 per cent for the lower ones. No adjustment has been made for rice yield in 1959-60, which may have been overestimated (see ftn. 13).

10. The purchase price of land was set at 2.5 times the standard output of the land established in 1948, in the present example, 9,735 kilograms (3,894 x 2.5). The annual payment for the total purchase price was based on the amortization table, Tang, op. cit., p. 211, according to which the total principal outstanding was 1,260,000,000 kilograms and the annual payment in two installments (2 x 75,600,000) was 151,200,000 kilograms. Since the principal is 2.5 times the annual output, we know that the annual output must be equal to 5,040 million kilograms. The annual payment of 151,200,000 kilograms is 30 per cent x 5,040 million kilograms.

11. In this connection, the three alternative sets of production figures mentioned earlier in the chapter show their difference. In terms of disposable income, the higher production figure in Table 14 results in 63 kilograms, while in the other two lower sets of figures, it is 4 kilograms and 5 kilograms, respectively. The difference in net receipts is 296 kilograms under one assumption and 343 kilograms under the other.

12. Taiwan Food Balance Sheet (JCRR). For a summary, see Basic Agricultural Statistics of Taiwan (Taipei: JCRR, 1962).

13. We take rice consumption per head to be 143 kilograms for 1959 and 1960, instead of the official estimates of 147 and 151 kilograms. The margin of error is, therefore, estimated to be about 4 per cent by the author.

14. The majority of farms have not allowed for adequate depreciation for irrigation works, farm implements, and residential buildings. On account of the general underestimation of depreciation charges, we shall rely on gross farm income instead of farm income.

15. See ftn. 13.

CHAPTER 5

1. Peter T. Bauer and Basil S. Yamey, The Economics of Underdeveloped Countries (Chicago: University of Chicago Press, 1957), p. 212.

2. D. G. Johnson, "Resources Allocation under Share Contracts," Journal of Political Economy, 58 (April, 1950), p. 119.

3. The theory has been expounded by many in one form or another. See R. Schickele, "Effect of Tenure Systems on Agricultural Efficiency," Journal of Farm Economics, XLII, (February, 1941), pp. 185-207, and E. O. Heady, "Economics of Farm Leasing," ibid., XXIX

(August, 1947), pp. 659–78. Here we try to restate it conveniently for organizing the empirical data in the sections that follow.

4.

Let $X = f(1, c, L)$ represent production function and $\qquad$ (1)
$Y = X - wl - ic - \alpha X$ represent the profit or income equation, $\qquad$ (2)
where X = output, 1 = units of labor, c = units of capital, L = units of land, w = wage rate, and i = interest rate.
Proportional rent is represented by $0 < \alpha < 1$. The units of X are chosen so that its price is equal to unity.

The problem is to maximize income Y subject to the production function. We set the partial derivitives of (2) with respect to 1 and c, respectively, on the assumption that input of land is fixed and equate them to zero.

$$\frac{\partial Y}{\partial 1} = \frac{\partial X}{\partial 1} - w - \alpha \frac{\partial X}{\partial 1} = 0 \qquad (3)$$

$$\frac{\partial Y}{\partial c} = \frac{\partial X}{\partial c} - \alpha \frac{\partial X}{\partial c} = 0 \qquad (4)$$

or

$$w = (1 - \alpha) \frac{\partial X}{\partial 1} \qquad (5)$$

$$i = (1 - \alpha) \frac{\partial X}{\partial c} \qquad (6)$$

Equations (5) and (6) show that labor and capital will be employed until the wage rate and interest rate are respectively equal to the value of the marginal product to the tenant, which is $(1-\alpha)$ of the actual value of marginal product. Thus, a reduction in α will give incentive to use more labor and capital to a given input of land. The assumption of a fixed land input is a realistic one in the present context. In Taiwan, the problem of varying the size of land for a tenant in order to maximize his income or profit is a remote possibility. The issue of land input as a variable was explored against the U.S. background by D.G. Johnson, op. cit., pp. 111–23.

If the tenants instead of hired hands work on the farm, the above conditions for maximum profit need a slight reformulation. In place of the income or profit function, we have a utility function:

$$U = g(s, Y) \qquad (7)$$

Here s denotes leisure and Y, income. Both income and leisure are desirable $\partial U / Y s > 0$, $\partial U / \partial Y > 0$. The rate of substitution of income for leisure is

$$-\frac{dY}{ds} = \frac{g_1}{g_2} \qquad (8)$$

By definition, $s = T - 1$ (9)

Here, T is the total available time. Substitute (2) after deleting wl and (9) into (7):

$$U = g\,[T - 1, (1-\alpha)\,X - ic]$$ (10)

To maximize utility set the derivitive of (10) with respect to 1 equal to zero:

$$\frac{\partial U}{\partial 1} = -g_1 + g_2\,\left[(1 - \partial)\,\frac{\partial X}{\partial 1}\right] = 0$$ (11)

and therefore: $$-\frac{dY}{ds} = \frac{g_1}{g_2} = (1-\alpha)\,\frac{\partial X}{\partial 1} = w$$ (12)

This states that the rate of substitution of income for leisure equals the value of marginal product of labor, which is the wage rate (w). Thus, a reduction of rent $(1-\alpha)$ will result in more effort on the part of tenants on the assumption that the utility function after land reform remains unchanged.

If the rent should be fixed, the term αX in (2) will be replaced by a constant which will disappear in the course of taking the derivatives of (2) with respect to c and 1. The effect is that labor and capital will be employed until the wage rate and interest rate are respectively equal to the value of marginal products to the tenant, which are: $\partial X/\partial 1$ and $\partial X/\partial c$ instead of $(1-\alpha)\,\partial X/\partial 1$ and $(1-\alpha)\,\partial X/\partial c$ (where $0<\alpha<1$), as in the case of proportional rent.

     5. See the number of days the farm workers spent on the farm and off the farm as estimated by the Rural Economic Division of JCRR and cited in Economic Bulletin for Asia and the Far East, XIV, No. 1, (June, 1963), p. 58.

     6.
Productivity of Aggregate Agricultural Input Index, 1901-60

Period	Productivity of Aggregate Input Index (1903 = 100)
1901–5	96.7
1906–10	95.9
1911–15	85.9
1916–20	86.6
1921–25	96.8
1926–30	107.2
1931–35	120.8
1936–40	126.8

Productivity of Aggregate Agricultural Input Index (continued)

Period	Productivity of Aggregate Input Index (1903 = 100)
1941-45	114.1
1946-50	111.6
1951-55	133.5
1956-60	159.8

See Yhi-min Ho, The Agricultural Development of Taiwan 1903-60 (Unpublished Ph.D. dissertation, Vanderbilt University, 1965), p. 109.

7. See Chapter 2.

8. If all inputs are included and factor shares used as weights, the exponents should add to unity. This method implies a special form of the Cobb-Douglas production function with no constant term, which will be accounted for later in connection with neutral technological change. The function is log-linear and homogenous of degree one. All factors are assumed to be paid their marginal products, i.e., the factor markets are competitive.

9. All factors are valued at the 1952-56 average factor prices. The total cost is calculated for a number of years selected at five-year intervals. The arithmetic means of each factor cost for these selected years is taken as the weight of factors or the exponent of the equation. Ho, op. cit., p. 103.

10. We combine working and fixed capital, i.e., X_{31} and X_{32}, into X_3. Ho's figures seem to be in line with the estimates made for a few other countries, as quoted by Anthony M. Tang in his "Policy and Performance in Agriculture" (to be included in a forthcoming volume on Economic Trends in Communist China), although international data are not strictly comparable.

Relative Input Weights of Selected Countries

Country	Year	Land	Labor	Capital	(including current inputs)
Japan *	1933-37	0.26	0.52	0.22	
India**	1945-48	0.25	0.34	0.41	
U.S.A.***	1949	0.19	0.33	0.48	

Source: * From A. M. Tang, "Research and Education in Japanese Agricultural Development, 1880-1938," The Economics Studies Quarterly (Riron Keizai Gaku, May, 1963), p. 93.
     ** From T. W. Schultz, Transforming Traditional Agriculture, (New Haven: Yale University Press, 1964), pp. 99-100. India's data pertain to Punjab.
     *** From Zui Griliches, "Sources of Measured Productivity Growth," Journal of Political Economy, 71 (August, 1963), p. 336.

11. The base year of $\bar{I}_t$ must be adjusted each time to coincide with that of the q_o. The formulation is based on R. M. Solow's "Technical Change and the Aggregate Production Function," Review of Economics and Statistics, 39 (August, 1957), pp. 312-20.

12. The total input data in Table 16 were based on estimates by JCRR. The capital-input index for the years 1954-60 are derived as follows:

Year	1954	1955	1956	1957	1958	1959	1960
Capital-input index	104	115	123	127	139	135	136

13. The formula for calculating the rates of technical progress is as follows:

$q'_t = q_t - I_t q_o$ (where all the symbols are explained in the text except for $(1 + r)^t$, which is the rate of technological progress, broadly defined).

Since $q_t/q_o = (1 + r)^t I_t$, we have $q'_t = (1 + r)^t I_t q_o - I_t q_o$ and solve for $(1 + r)$.

14. Yhi-min Ho, op. cit., p. 120.

15. See ftn. 10.

16. Taiwan Agricultural Yearbook (1961), p. 32.

17.
Average Brown Rice Production per Hectare, 1900-1959
(Unit: Kilogram)

Period	First Crop	Change	Second Crop	Change	Average	Change
1900-1904	1,373	81	1,056	207	1,209	144
1905-09	1,454	4	1,263	- 40	1,353	23
1910-14	1,458	123	1,223	52	1,330	83
1915-19	1,581	85	1,275	36	1,413	55
1920-24	1,666	92	1,311	242	1,468	174
1925-29	1,758	258	1,553	98	1,642	166
1930-34	2,016	202	1,651	268	1,808	244
1935-39	2,218	-211	1,919	-279	2,052	-223
1940-44	2,067	-379	1,640	-294	1,829	-340
1945-49	1,688	465	1,346	538	1,489	514
1950-54	2,153	472	1,884	204	2,003	319
		407		169		270
1955-59	2,625		2,088		2,322	

Source: Taiwan Food Statistics Book (1961), see Appendix Table 2.

18.

Rice Yields in Major Producing Countries: Changes from 1935-39 to 1960-62

Country	Change From 1935-39 to 1960-62		Annual Compound Rate of Change	
	Per Cent	Rank *	Per Cent	Rank*
United States	+ 56	1	+1.9	1
Brazil	+ 12	9 1/2	+0.5	7 1/3
U.A.R. (Egypt)	+ 22	4	+0.8	4
Malagasy Republic	- 5	11	-0.2	9
Burma	+ 16	7	+ 0.6	6
China (Taiwan)	+ 25	3	+ 0.9	3
India	+ 17	6	+ 0.7	5 1/2
Indonesia	+ 13	8	+ 0.5	7 1/3
Japan	+ 26	2	+ 1.0	2
Korea (South)	+ 18	5	+ 0.7	5 1/2
Pakistan	+ 12	9 1/2	+ 0.5	7 1/3
Philippines	+ 7	10	+ 0.3	8
Thailand	- 8	12	-0.3	10

* The ranks are inserted by the present author. The percentage change calculations are based on unrounded yield figures.

Source: L. R. Brown, Increasing World Food Output Problems and Prospects (Foreign Agriculture Economic Report, No. 25, USDA 1965), p. 42.

19. The farmers in Taiwan are faced with a less profitable fertilizer-cost/rice-price relationship than those in Japan, not to mention the United States. The effect of this unfavorable price serves to reduce the amount of fertilizer used and, hence, the potential for raising the yields. Yet, the margin of the annual compound rate of change of yield in Japan for the period of the 1930's to the 1960's was only 1 per cent above that in Taiwan. The incentive effect of the land reform would have been more markedly reflected in the productivity figures had the fertilizer-rice price been more favorable to the farmers.

20.

Average Brown Rice Production per Hectare, 1900-1959 (Paddy Versus Upland) (Unit: Kilograms)

Period	Paddy Rice	Change	Upland Rice	Change
1900-1904	1,253	135	750	241
1905-09	1,388	- 14	991	-117

Average Brown Rice Production per Hectare (continued)

Period	Paddy Rice	Change	Upland Rice	Change
1910-14	1,374	87	874	27
1915-19	1,461	63	901	25
1920-24	1,524	157	926	165
1925-29	1,681	163	1,091	180
1930-34	1,844	253	1,271	- 69
1935-39	2,097	-233	1,202	-452
1940-44	1,864	-333	750	9
1945-49	1,531	543	759	240
1950-54	2,074	302	999	- 4
		279		-207
1955-59	2,376		995	

Source: See Appendix Table 2.

21.

Average Production per Hectare of Sweet Potatoes and Peanuts, 1900-1959
(Unit: Kilogram)

Period	Sweet Potato	Change	Peanut	Change
1900-1904	5,935	1,246	529	104
1905-09	7,181	- 561	633	-124
1910-14	6,620	627	509	213
1915-19	7,247	764	722	23
1920-24	8,011	1,775	745	113
1925-29	9,786	1,142	858	37
1930-34	10,928	1,015	858	64
1935-39	11,943	-1,633	959	-220
1940-44	10,310	-1,777	739	- 71
1945-49	8,533	670	668	47
1950-54	9,203	2,511	715	152
		-229		-92
1955-59	11,714		867	

Source: See Appendix Tables 3 and 4.

22. See ftn. 21.

23.
Average Production per Hectare of Sugar Cane, 1902-59
(Unit: Kilogram)

Period	Sugar Cane	Change
1902-04 (2 years)	28,184	1,879
1905-09	30,063	-4,227
1910-14	25,836	7,212
1915-19	33,408	-2,588
1920-24	30,820	19,148
1925-29	49,968	16,978
1930-34	66,946	3,387
1935-39	70,333	-10,519
1940-44	59,814	-23,772
1945-49	36,042	20,436
1950-54	56,478	18,667
1955-59	75,145	4,812

Source: Economic History of Taiwan Under the Japanese Control (in Chinese), I, pp. 41-42, and Taiwan Agricultural Yearbook (1962), p. 5.

24. This statement is subject to some reservation because of the possible effects of weather cycles on the agriculture production. Our data covering sixty years are too short to isolate such an impact.

25. In his study on the agriculture productivity, a leading agricultural scientist, Dr. Shen, concluded that "fertilizer has been a major cause of increased rice production . . . for sweet potatoes, peanuts . . ., only a small percentage of the planted acreage is fertilized, although production can be greatly raised through increased application of fertilizers." T. H. Shen, Agricultural Development on Taiwan Since World War II (Ithaca, N.Y.: Comstock Publishing Associates, 1964), p. 138.

26. Basic Statistics of Agricultural Labor and Employment in Taiwan (JCRR, February, 1963).

27. See T. H. Shen, op. cit., pp. 176-95, for an extended discussion of the history of evolution of rice varieties and crop system in Taiwan.

28.   Size of Holdings and Yield of Paddy Rice 1958-62*

Unit: Catty (0.59682 kilogram)

	1958[1]		1959[2]		1960[3]		1961[3]	
	First Crop	Second Crop	First Crop	Second Crop	First Crop	Second Crop	First Crop	Second Crop
Under 0.49 chia	7,172	6,264	7,810	6,742	9,489	8,011	7,432	6,880
0.50-0.99 chia	6,821	6,432	5,212	3,314	7,367	6,423	6,859	5,790
1.00-1.49 chia	6,726	5,984	6,136	5,762	6,861	5,870	6,636	5,400
1.50-1.99 chia	5,821	5,754	4,719	4,872	6,001	5,074	6,086	4,789
Above 2.00 chia	5,707	5,492	4,705	4,313	6,419	5,249	6,258	5,350

*Size of Sample

	1958	Percentage	1959	Percentage	Percentage for Sample Census of 1956
Under 0.49 chia	19	4.52	13	6.22	34.39
0.50-0.99 chia	59	14.05	40	19.14	28.43
1.00-1.49 chia	94	22.38	49	23.44	16.44
1.50-1.99 chia	72	17.14	34	16.27	9.10
Above 2.00 chia	176	41.91	73	34.93	11.64
	420	100	209	100	100

Sources: [1]Preliminary Report on the Farm Account in Taiwan 1958 (Department of Agriculture and Forestry, Provincial Government of Taiwan, October, 1959).

[2]Preliminary Report on the Farm Account in Taiwan 1959 (Department of Agriculture and Forestry, Provincial Government of Taiwan, June, 1961).

[3]Copied from Preliminary Report on the Farm Account in Taiwan, 1960 and 1961 (Department of Agriculture and Forestry, Provincial Government of Taiwan, unpublished).

29. There is the question of the representativeness of the sample. For 1958 and 1959, we have the distribution of observations among holdings of various sizes. A comparison of their percentage distribution with that of the sample census of 1956 shows that sample observations under 0.49 chia are not adequately represented in the 1958 and 1959 farm account surveys.

30. The explanation was pointed out to me by Dr. J. Lossing Buck, who based his observations on the farm conditions on mainland China.

31. C. K. Wu and T. K. Lee, The Demand for and Supply of Farm Labor of the Families of the Vocational Students (in Chinese) (Taichung: Chung Hsin University, 1963), pp. 7-8.

32. W. A. Lewis, in his discussion of the weakness and merits of small-scale agriculture, lists points in favor of the small-size farms. Small farmers cultivate land more intensively and carefully than large farmers. Small-scale farming does not make much demand upon supervisory staff. He quoted Arthur Young, who, after observing the French peasantry, said: "The magic of property turns sand into gold," The Theory of Economic Growth (Homewood, Illinois: Richard D. Irwin, 1955), p. 134. Evidence in Italy [Land Reform in Italy: Achievements and Perspectives (Food and Agriculture Organization of the U.N., 1961)] and Taiwan lend support to this.

33. Op. cit., p. 119.

34. What is of interest is that such an assumption is sufficient, but not necessary; that is, even without assuming a change of the preference map between income and work as holdings vary, one can still demonstrate that small landholders may put in more labor after the reduction of the size of their holdings, provided the indifference curves are of appropriate curvature between income and work.

35. Wu and Lee, op. cit., p. 12.

CHAPTER 6

1. For the individual exchange ratios, see Food Production and Activities of the Taiwan Food Bureau (1962), p. 25.

2. C. S. Shih, L. Lin, and L. M. Kou, "An Appraisal of the Fertilizer-Rice Barter System in Taiwan," Journal of Social Science (in Chinese) (June, 1961), pp. 238 and 240.

3. Ibid., p. 241.

4. Taiwan Statistical Data Book (Taipei, 1962), p. 91.

5. As a check for the procedure, we find that the gain under the detailed calculation for 1959 is NT$404 million, while the rough approximate estimation yields the figure of NT$397 million with an error of about 2 per cent. Thus, the figures in Table 23 follow the crude method of estimation as far as the gains for fertilizer barter are concerned.

6. Simon Kuznets, "Economic Growth and the Contribution of Agriculture: Notes on Measurements," International Journal of Agrarian Affairs, 3, (April, 1961), pp. 59-75, reprinted in C. K. Eicher and L. W. Witt, Agriculture in Economic Development (New York: McGraw-Hill, 1964), pp. 102-24.

7. Ibid., p. 116.

8.

National Income, Savings, and Growth Rate, 1951-61
(Unit: millions of NT$)

	(1)	(2)	(3)	(4)	(5)
	National Income				
Year	(Current Price)	(1952 Price)	Growth Rate (Per Cent)	Savings (Current Price)	Savings (4) as Percentage of (1)
1951	8,942	11,528		1,482	16.57
1952	13,047	13,047	13.2	2,249	17.24
1953	17,882	15,023	15.1	2,732	15.28
1954	18,807	15,631	4.0	2,182	11.60
1955	22,561	16,602	6.2	3,238	14.35
1956	26,041	17,505	5.4	2,373	9.11
1957	29,982	18,672	6.7	2,945	9.82
1958	32,827	19,716	5.6	4,394	13.39
1959	38,513	21,073	6.9	5,136	13.34
1960	48,008	22,661	7.5	7,544	15.71
1961	53,726	24,547	8.4	n.a.	...
Average			7.90		13.64

Source: Taiwan Statistical Data Book (1962), p. 12.
National Income of the Republic of China (Taipei: Directorate-General of Budgets, Accounts and Statistics, Executive Yuan, 1962).

9.

Income and Growth Rates of Agriculture and Nonagriculture Sectors 1951-60
(Unit: Millions in 1952 constant NT$)

Year	(1) Agriculture Forestry, Hunting and Fishing	(2) Growth Rate (Per Cent)	(3) Nonagri- culture Sector	(4) Growth Rate (Per Cent)	(5) (1) as Per- centage of Total National Income
1951	3,989		7,539		36.26
1952	4,878	22.29	8,169	8.36	37.39
1953	6,816	39.73	8,207	0.47	41.46
1954	5,992	-12.09	9,639	17.41	35.47
1955	6,349	5.96	10,253	6.37	35.75
1956	6,356	0.11	11,149	8.74	34.94
1957	6,652	4.66	12,020	7.81	34.06
1958	7,035	5.76	12,681	5.50	33.36
1959	7,224	2.69	13,849	9.21	32.35
1960	8,831	22.25	13,830	-0.14	36.22
Average		10.15		7.08	35.73

Source: Same as in ftn. 8.

10. Ibid.

11. Ibid.

12. For a cogent argument for the contribution of agricultural credit in economic development, see Horace Belshaw, Agricultural Credit in Economically Underdeveloped Countries (Rome: Food and Agriculture Organization, 1959).

13. Arthur W. Peterson, An Economic Study of Land Use in Taichung Hsien and City, 1960 (Taichung, Taiwan: Research Institute of Agricultural Economics, Chung Hsing University, 1962), as quoted in E. L. Rada and T. H. Lee, Irrigation Investment in Taiwan, (Taipei: JCRR, 1963), p. 29.

14. Taiwan Statistical Data Book, pp. 17-18.

15. Ibid.

16. The argument in this section is largely a digest and partial summary of S. C. Tsiang's Suggestions for a Reconsideration of the Interest Rate and Banking Policy (in Chinese) (Taipei: The International Economic Information Center, 1959).

17. An official justification for pegging the rate is that this reduces the cost of producers and accordingly the price of products from the subsidized producers. However, in a competitive market, prices are determined by the cost of producing the marginal unit of output (marginal cost, not the average cost). If the public and private enterprises and farmers cannot satisfy all their requirements for loans from the official sources, they have to borrow from private moneylenders. According to one estimate, the farmers obtain more than 40 per cent of their total credit requirements from private moneylenders. (Based on a survey of farm family finance, by the Provincial Bureau of Agriculture and Forestry (1960), as quoted in N. C. Loh, "Taiwan's Farm Finance," Bank of Taiwan Quarterly (in Chinese), 13, No. 3 (September, 1962), p.12. Should this be true, the arbitrarily low rate has no effect at all on their marginal cost and, hence, on their prices. Low interest rate loans then become a form of subsidy to the few fortunate borrowers who are able to get them.

18. Exceptions to the statement are 1954 and 1960.

19. The example is due to Tsiang, op. cit. Assume that the national income of Taiwan is $100, of which $90 is consumed and $10 saved by the domestic residents. If one half of the domestic savings is used to finance the consumption of foreign residents in Taiwan, only half of the current domestic savings is then available to finance domestic investment. The national income account would be:

$$\text{National income} = \text{Consumption} + \text{Investment}$$
$$\$100 = (\$90 + \$5) + \$5$$

If none of the current savings were used to buy foreign currency notes, the foreigners would have to finance their consumption expenditures in Taiwan either with imports of the same value to raise the proceeds in local currency or by selling a corresponding amount of foreign exchange to the banks, which, in turn, would be able to finance an equal amount of additional imports in excess of the exports. The national income account would then be:

$$\text{National income} = \text{Consumption} + \text{Investment} - \text{Import Surplus}$$
$$\$100 = [(\$90 + \$5) + \$10 - \$5].$$

20. Shih, Lin, and Kou, op. cit., p. 20.

CHAPTER 7

1. For a recent survey of the literature, see C. K. Eicher and L. W. Witt, (eds.), Agriculture in Economic Development (New York: McGraw-Hill, 1964), pp. 129-44.

2. J. Robinson, "Disguised Unemployment," Economic Journal, 46 (June, 1936), pp. 225-37, reprinted in Essays in the Theory of Employment (London: Oxford University Press, 1947), pp. 82-107.

3. Viner, on the other hand, questions whether this situation will ever be reached. He said: "I find it impossible to conceive a farm of any kind on which, other factors of production being held constant in quantity, and even in form as well, it would not be possible, by known methods, to obtain some addition to the crop by using additional labor in more careful selection and planting of the seed, more intensive weeding, cultivation, thinning, and mulching, more painstaking harvesting, gleaning and cleaning of the crop." See J. Viner, "Some Reflections on the Concept of Disguised Unemployment," in Contribucoes a Analise do Desenvolvimento (Rio de Janeiro, 1957), p. 347.

4. See Liu Su Feng, Disguised Unemployment in Taiwan Agriculture (Unpublished Ph.D. dissertation, University of Illinois, 1966).

He used the production function analysis to test the hypothesis that the annual marginal productivity of labor was zero, and he found that on the average, the marginal value product of farm labor in Taiwan during the period 1961-63 was positive (Chapter 4). By using the same set of farm record data, he also found, by the labor utilization method, that although in some regions during 1961-62 there existed a chronic visible underemployment of family labor, there was a shortage of family labor in July throughout the period of 1961-62 (Chapter 5).

5. Ibid., pp. 181-85.

6. In what follows, the data will be given a theoretical rationalization. In Figure 4 the quantity of farm labor is measured along OX' and value product along XY. Off-farm labor units 00' are treated as a fixed quantity because they are largely determined by the availability of job opportunities rather than by other considerations, as shown in Table 26. Assuming that capital input remains constant for simplicity of graphic demonstration, we have a family of total product curves of labor. The position or height of each curve is determined by the size of landholdings. It is assumed that no labor will be applied beyond the zero product point. In other words, we assume that MPP, and, accordingly, MVP, are positive. The assumption explains the flat portion of the total product curve of labor near the Y axis. The amount of labor input at equilibrium will depend upon the utility of income versus

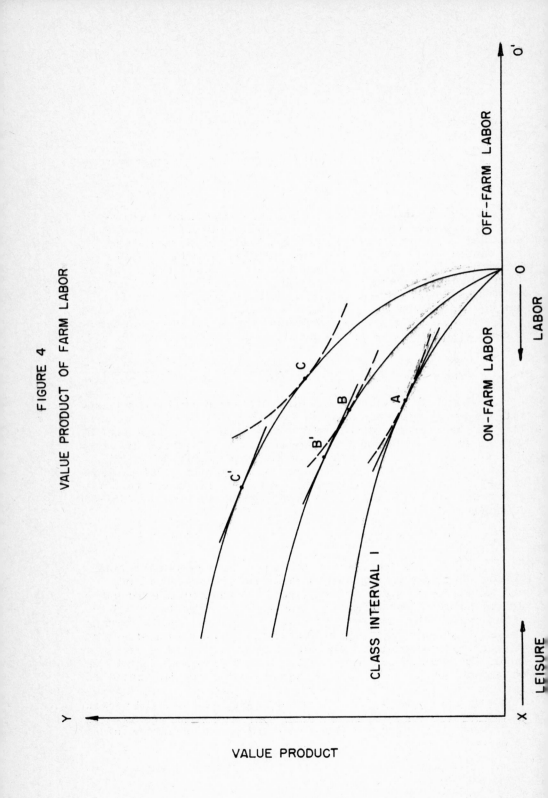

FIGURE 4

VALUE PRODUCT OF FARM LABOR

172

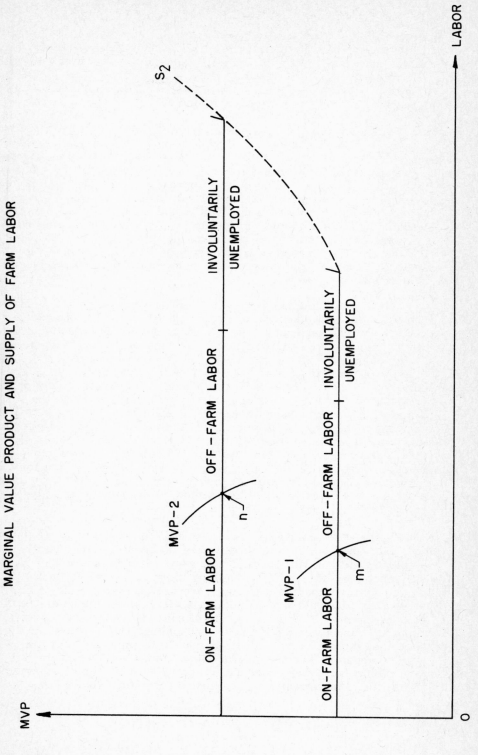

FIGURE 5

MARGINAL VALUE PRODUCT AND SUPPLY OF FARM LABOR

173

leisure of the farm family, on the one hand, and labor productivity, on the other. A representative family of constant utility (indifference) curves is drawn. At equilibrium, MVP should be equal to the marginal rate of substitution between leisure and income, i.e., the point of tangency between the total product curve and the indifference curve. A few such points are marked A, B, and C.

For the purpose of illustration, let the lowest total product curve represent land input in the first group (0.4999 chia, or less). The slope of a line drawn through A (tangent to both the indifference curve and the total product curve) will show the MVP of labor at that point. Draw a family of such parallel lines tangent to the total product curves at points B′ and C′ in order to compare whether B and C are to the left or right of B′ and C′ at various intervals of landholdings. This graphic procedure capitalizes on the concavity of the total product curve. In our diagram, B and C are to the right of B′ and C′. This means that, theoretically, it is not inconceivable for MVP of labor to increase at the new equilibrium points, when the holding size gets larger.

What we just said can be restated in the framework of demand and supply analysis. We know that given the land input, MVP of labor curve describes what happens to the marginal output when each additional labor input is applied. With each increase of landholding, the MVP curve of labor will shift to the right. We postulate that the supply function of labor from each farm family is horizontal until it reaches a point of 76.99 per cent of labor utilization. From that point on, the curve bends upward. For a family with a large holding, the supply curve of labor may bend backward beyond the zero elasticity point, presumably because of income effect. This is, of course, a theoretical idealization made to simplify our analysis, but not entirely without justification. For example, Wonnacott derived an aggregate supply function of labor of the same shape as the one we postulate for each individual farm. [See Paul Wonnacott, "Disguised and Overt Unemployment in Underdeveloped Economies," Quarterly Journal of Economics 76 (May, 1962), pp. 279-97.]

In Figure 5 the vertical axis measures MVP of labor and the horizontal axis the labor units. The three parts of labor supply, namely, units employed on the farm, off the farm, as well as unemployed, are marked off separately for each landholding class. The usual concave MVP curves (with respect to the origin) are drawn. Take the curve labelled MVP-1 to illustrate a hypothetical MVP curve of labor for the farm size in interval 1. It is to the left of curve 2 because curve 2 represents MVP of labor with a larger landholding. The MVP curves intersect the supply curves of labor at points m and n indicating what would happen to the quantity of labor demanded and supplied as the landholding increases from one class to the next. Point n is slightly higher than m because the earlier discussion indicates a possible higher MVP of labor with landholding in interval 2 than in interval 1. The difference may not be too noticeable in view of a possibly infinitesimal change. However, when the absolute amount of labor supplied starts to decrease when the size holding increases (as shown in interval 11 of Table 26), the MVP at that interval must be noticeably higher than that at intervals, say, 1 or 2. The observation is based on Figure 4, i.e., the slope of a line passing the tangency point C is steeper than that at points A or B. The scale in Figure 5 is magnified for the purpose of illustration. Through institutional rigidity of keeping jobs in the family, such differences in MVP can remain among various landholding class intervals. The available supply function of labor, S_2 in Figure 3, is derived by joining the end points of the horizontal portions of the supply function of each group.

7. The figures in Column 7 can be calculated alternatively by multiplying the corresponding figures in Columns 5 and 3.

8. Wu and Lee, op. cit., p. 13.

9. P. N. Rosenstein-Rodan observed that "more than 10 per cent of the active labor force in southern Italian agriculture is surplus . . ." in "Disguised Unemployment and Underemployment in Agriculture," Monthly Bulletin of Agricultural Economics and Statistics, 6, (Rome: FAO, July–August, 1957). Later Berdj Kenadjian reported, after having discussed this point with Rosenstein-Rodan: "When Rosenstein-Rodan observes that in southern Italy around 10 to 12 per cent of the actual population in agriculture are removable, he is including among the removable surplus the individuals who are needed for 50 days or less. If the more rigid definition, which is also the more sensible one, is adopted, the removable surplus is reduced to 5 per cent." Disguised Unemployment in Underdeveloped Countries (Unpublished Ph.D. dissertation, Harvard University, 1957), p. 250, as quoted in C. K. Eicher and L. W. Witt, op. cit., p. 139.

10. Liu, op. cit., p. 185.

11. D. G. Johnson, "Comparability of Labor Capacities of Farm and Non-Farm Labor," American Economic Review 43 (June, 1953); "Functioning of the Labor Market," Journal of Farm Economics 33 (February, 1951); T. W. Schultz, Economic Organization of Agriculture (New York: McGraw-Hill, 1953), pp. 285-86.

12.

Per Capita Income of Labor in Agriculture and Other Economic Sectors
(Unit: NT$)

Year	(1) Agriculture	(2) Industry	(3) Commerce and Others	(4) Relative Income (1)/(2)	(5) Relative Income (1)/(3)
1951	1,694	7,427	4,836	0.23	0.35
1952	2,564	8,441	7,063	0.30	0.36
1953	3,888	10,996	9,024	0.35	0.43
1954	3,462	11,945	10,099	0.29	0.34
1955	4,163	14,645	11,642	0.28	0.36
1956	4,738	17,812	13,371	0.27	0.35
1957	5,318	20,118	14,250	0.26	0.37
1958	5,738	20,414	15,102	0.28	0.38
1959	6,351	24,006	17,101	0.26	0.37
1960	8,732	26,854	19,724	0.33	0.44
1961	9,772	29,328	20,971	0.33	0.47

Source: Basic Statistics of Agricultural Labor and Employment in Taiwan (Compiled by the Rural Economic Division JCCR, February, 1963), Table 3.

13. In a sample survey of 1,383 urban households in 1953, about three fifths of those interviewed had lived where they live now for ten years or less. Still another measure of the rapid rate of urbanization in the Taiwan cities is the age at which these newcomers came to the city. Two thirds of the heads of households and three fourths of the wives not born in the city moved to the city between the ages of sixteen and thirty-five years.

14. Arthur F. Raper, Rural Taiwan—Problems and Promise (Taipei: JCRR, July, 1953), p. 254.

The survey was made in late 1952 in sixteen townships. Three villages within the township were selected. From the three villages so chosen, approximately seventy-five households were subject to detailed interviews, making a total of 1,176 households interviewed.

15. E. Stuart Kirby, Rural Progress in Taiwan (Taipei: JCRR, December, 1960). Eighteen townships were selected for study in the 1959 survey of which sixteen were the same as in the 1952 survey. The two townships were added because one showed the effect of new industries and the other of new crops on rural life.

16. Ibid., p. 121.

17. Ibid., p. 121.

18.

Children of Farmer Purchasers Receiving
Education in Schools
(Unit: Number of Persons)

Year	Primary School	Secondary School	College
1948	140,461	5,589	0
1953	268,899	19,590	413
1957	324,299	35,400	422
1961	433,790	61,523	1602

Source: Data collected at exhibits showing the Achievements of Land
Reform in Taiwan, 1962.

19. I owe this conjecture to Professor M. Bronfenbrenner.

20. The number of tractors used on the farm in the intervening
years is as follows:

Year	Number	Year	Number
1955	9	1958	510
1956	60	1959	2,262
1957	180	1960	3,708

Source: Plant Industry Division, JCRR.

21. Lester R. Brown, Increasing World Food-Output Problems
and Prospects (Foreign Agricultural Economic Report No. 25, n.s.
Department of Agriculture, 1965), pp. 34-46.

22. Ibid., p. vii.

23. C. Cheng, Land Reform in Taiwan (Taipei: China Publishing
Co., 1961), p. 314.

24. Bernard Gallin, "Land Reform in Taiwan: Its Effect on
Rural Social Organization and Leadership," Human Organization, 22,
No. 3 (Summer, 1963), pp. 109-12.

25. David N. Rowe, "Land Tenure and Social Stability in Asia:
United States Policy Problems," in Walter Froehlich, (ed.), Land
Tenure Industrialization and Social Stability (Milwaukee: Marquette
University Press, 1961), p. 29.

26. See Appendix Table 9.

27. L. P. Chow and S. C. Hsu, "Statistical Studies on Mortality Changes in Taiwan During the Last Decade," Industry of Free China, XIV, No. II (August, 1960).

28. Shao-hsing Chen, Tao-tung Wang, and F. J. Foley, "Pattern of Fertility in Taiwan-Report of a Survey Made in 1957," Journal of Social Science, 13 (Taipei: National Taiwan University, 1963), pp. 209-94.

29. The cross-sectional fertility rates for 1948-57 for the Taiwanese are: Taipei, 6.586; suburb, 6.566; fishing village, 7.917; and farming village, 7.243; and for the mainlanders, 5.265. See Shao-hsing Chen, ibid., pp. 232-33.

30. The average fertility rate for the Taiwanese in Taipei and suburb is 6.576 per cent. Since most of the mainlanders, which form roughly one fifth of the population, reside in the cities, a weighted average for the urban fertility rate is estimated to be 6.31 per cent. Similarly, the population in the fishing villages constitutes a small fraction of the total agricultural population, and we assign a weight of one tenth to the fertility rate of the fishing village and secure a weighted average of 7.31 per cent for the rural fertility rate. Thus, we estimate that the rural fertility rate is 0.5 per cent above the simple average of the urban-rural rate, 6.81 per cent, since the agricultural population is about one half of the total population (Appendix Table 9). The net growth rate in the rural area is to be reduced by 0.1 per cent from the average of 3.6 per cent for the island because of the higher death rate and raised by 0.5 per cent because of the higher fertility rate, making an adjusted net rate of 4.0 per cent. The higher fertility rate in the rural area is largely due to the earlier marriage of women and longer period of procreation. Among the Taiwanese women, the mean age of first marriage is about nineteen in urban settlements and eighteen in the rural area. The mean number of years between the first and last birth is 13.81 in Taipei, 15.26 in the suburb, 17.63 in the farming village, and 19.31 in the fishing village. Ibid., p. 47.

31. The projection, based on a series of agricultural population figures, presumably stops in 1959 because the series beginning in 1960 represents an abrupt change from the old. There was no explanation of how such a sudden change in the agricultural population took place in 1960.

32. See the data collected in Colin Clark's Conditions of Economic Progress (2nd ed.; London: Macmillan, 1951).

CHAPTER 8

1. This brief mention of the work of JCRR is no true measure of its contributions. On the contrary, JCRR has touched on so many aspects of agricultural development that it requires a history of its own to do justice to it, and would certainly go beyond the scope of the present study.

2. H. S. Tang, Land Reform in Free China (Taipei: JCRR, 1954), p. 22.

3.

Economic Development Expenses at the
Provincial, County, and Village Levels
(Unit: Millions of new Taiwan dollars)

Year	Provincial		County	Village	Total	
	Total	Irrigation Investment			Current NT$	1949 Constant NT$
1949	7.6	. . .	11.8	...	19.4	19.4
1950	29.9	(0.5)	43.6	12.7	86.2	31.9
1951	35.8	(14.9)	79.9	19.5	135.2	30.2
1952	219.6	(24.0)	117.0	77.5	414.1	73.3
1953	220.0	(26.4)	171.3	117.6	508.9	85.0
1954	134.4	(27.5)	89.1	68.7	292.2	45.1
1955	148.4	(37.8)	112.3	70.0	330.7	47.3
1956	170.8	(41.1)	135.0	65.8	371.6	47.2
1957	204.3	(20.7)	148.8	79.9	433.0	51.3
1958	214.7	(56.8)	179.9	55.0	449.6	52.5
1959*						
1960*	367.7	(26.0)	111.0	63.0	541.7	53.3
1961	331.6	(n.a.)	136.8	63.0	532.9	47.6
						586.7

*Change from calendar to fiscal year. The 1959-60 data are from July 1, 1959, to June 30, 1960.

Source: Development of Taiwan 1945-62 (in Chinese) (Provincial Bureau of Information, 1962), Chapter V.

For figures on irrigation investment, see E. L. Rada and T. H. Lee, Irrigation Investment in Taiwan (Taipei: JCRR, 1963), p. 136. Conversion was made into 1949 constant new Taiwan dollars.

4. Suppose that the proportion of investment expenditure that must be spent on imports is a per cent and that the proportion of consumption on imports which would have occured if the saving had not been made is b per cent. The balance of payments will then be deteriorated by the saving and investment if a per cent is greater than b per cent and improve if b per cent is greater than a per cent. The size of a per cent does indeed depend upon the investment plan and may vary substantially from one type of project to another.

5. Taiwan Statistical Data Book (1962), Tables 10-3 and 10-4.

6. J. Hirshleifer, "On the Theory of Optimal Investment Decision," Journal of Political Economy, 66 (August, 1958), reprinted in E. Solomon, (ed.), Management of Corporate Capital, (Glencoe, Ill.: Free Press, 1959), pp. 205-28.

7. S. Kuznets, "Toward a Theory of Economic Growth," in Robert Lekachmen, (ed.), National Policy for Economic Welfare at Home and Abroad (New York: Doubleday and Co., Columbia University Bicentennial Conference Series, 1955), reprinted in S. Kuznets, Economic Growth and Structure (New York: W. W. Norton & Co., 1965), p. 36.

8. Y. C. Tsui, A Summary Report on Farm Income of Taiwan in 1957 in Comparison with 1952 (Taipei: JCRR, December, 1959), p. 44.

9. See Economic Bulletin for Asia and the Far East, XIV, No. 1 (June, 1963), p. 69.

10. S. Kuznets observed that one feature of economic growth common to all countries is an agricultural revolution, which he considered an indispensable early element. See "Present Underdeveloped Countries and Post-Growth Pattern," in Economic Growth and Structure (New York: W. W. Norton & Co., 1965), p. 191.

11. L. R. Brown, Increasing World Food-Output Problems and Prospects (Foreign Agricultural Economic Report No: 25, n.s. Department of Agriculture, 1965), pp. 52-58.

SELECTED BIBLIOGRAPHY

SELECTED BIBLIOGRAPHY

Chang, Han-Yu, and Myers, R. H. "Japanese Colonial Development Policy in Taiwan, 1895-1906: A Case Study of Bureaucratic Entrepreneurship," Journal of Asian Studies, XVII (August, 1963).

Chen, C. Land Reform in Taiwan (Taipei: China Publishing Company, 1961).

Ho, Samuel, P. S. "The Development Alternatives: The Case of Taiwan," Yale Economic Essays, No. 1 (Spring, 1965).

Ho, Yhi-min. The Agricultural Development of Taiwan 1903-60, unpublished Ph.D. dissertation, Vanderbilt University, 1965.

Kao, Charles H. C. The Role of The Agricultural Sector in Taiwan's Economic Development, unpublished Ph.D. dissertation, Michigan State University, 1964.

Kirby, E. S. Rural Progress in Taiwan (Taipei: JCRR, 1960).

Liu, Su Feng. Disguised Unemployment in Taiwan Agriculture, unpublished Ph.D. dissertation, University of Illinois, 1966.

Myers, R. H., and Ching, A. "Agricultural Development in Taiwan Under Japanese Control," Journal of Asian Studies, XXIII (August, 1964).

Rada, E. L., and Lee, T. H. Irrigation Investment in Taiwan (Taipei: JCRR, 1963).

Raper, A. F. Rural Taiwan—Problems and Promise (Taipei: JCRR, 1953).

Shen, T. H. Agricultural Development on Taiwan Since World War II (Ithaca, N.Y.: Comstock Publishing Associates, 1964).

Shih, C. S., Lin, L., and Kou, L. M. "An Appraisal of the Fertilizer-Rice Barter System in Taiwan," Journal of Social Science (in Chinese) (June, 1961).

Tang, H. S. Land Reform in Free China (Taipei: JCRR, 1954).

Tang, H. S., and Hsieh, S. C. "Land Reform and Agricultural Development in Taiwan," in Walter Froehlich (ed.), Land Tenure, Industrialization and Social Stability (Milwaukee: Wisconsin: Marquette University Press, 1961).

United Nations. "Relationship Between Agricultural and Industrial Development: A Case Study in Taiwan, China, 1953-1960," Economic Bulletin for Asia and the Far East, XIV, No. 1 (June, 1963).

Wu, C. K., and Lee, T. D. The Demand for and Supply of Farm Labor of the Families of the Vocational Students (in Chinese) (Taichung: Chung Hsin University, 1963).

INDEXES

NAME INDEX

Adelman, I., 145

Bauer, Peter T., 158
Belshaw, Horace, 169
Berguson, A. (Burk), 145
Bronfenbrenner, M., 177
Brown, Lester R., 163, 177, 180
Buchanan, N. S., 145
Buck, J. Lossing. 167

Chang, C. H., 141
Chang, Han-Yu, 146, 147
Chen, Shao-hsing, 178
Chen, Y. T., 79
Cheng, C., 34, 39, 152, 153, 177
Chiang, Monlin, 114, 124-25
Ching, A., 147
Chow, L. P., 178
Clark, Colin, 178

Eicher, C. K., 145, 168, 171, 175
Ellis, H. S., 145

Foley, F. J., 178
Froehlich, Walter, 153, 177

Gallin, Bernard, 177
Grajdanzer, Andrew J., 150
Griliches, Zui, 161

Heady, E. O., 158
Hirschleifer, J., 180
Ho, Ping-ti, 146, 151
Ho, Yhi-min, 67, 162
Hsieh, Chiao-min, 145
Hsieh, S. C., 57, 59, 153, 155
Hsu, S. C., 178

Johnson, B., 139
Johnson, D. G., 74, 158, 159, 175

Kenadjian, Berdj, 175
Kindleberger, Charles P., 150
Kirby, E. Stuart, 176
Kou, L. M., 167, 170

Kuznets, Simon, 83, 85, 120, 168, 180

Lee, T. H., 14, 79, 83, 104, 136, 153, 169, 179
Lee, T. K., 94, 96, 97, 167, 175
Lewis, W. A., 145, 167
Li, C. C., 141
Lin, L., 167, 170
Liu, Su Feng, 171, 175
Loh, N. C., 170

Marshall, Alfred, 145
Mears, L., 145
Mill, John Stuart, 145
Myers, R. H., 146, 147

Papanek, Gustav F., 145
Pepelasis, A., 145
Peterson, Arthur W., 169

Rada, E. L., 14, 83, 136, 153, 169, 179
Raper, Arthur F., 176
Raup, Philip M., 145
Robinson, Joan, 92, 97, 171
Rosenstein-Rodan, P. N., 175
Rowe, David N., 177

Schickele, R., 158
Schultz, T. W., 161, 175
Shen, T. H., 29, 152, 165
Shih, C. S., 167, 170
Smith, Adam, 145
Solomon, E., 180
Solow, R. M., 162

Tang, A. M., 161
Tang, H. S., 57, 59, 152, 153, 154, 155, 156, 179
Tsiang, S. C., 170
Tsui, Y. C., 180

Viner, J., 171

187

189

ABOUT THE AUTHOR

Anthony Y. C. Koo, Professor of Economics at Michigan State University, gained firsthand knowledge of the land reform program in Taiwan through three field trips to Taiwan during the last few years, including a nine-month stay in 1962-63.

From 1946-50, Professor Koo was technical counsellor of the Chinese Delegation to the Far Eastern Commission and responsible for matters related to reparations from Japan and economic and financial affairs of Japan. Prior to joining Michigan State in 1967, he was Professor of Economics at the University of Michigan. Since he joined the academic profession in 1950, he has written many articles on economic theory and international trade.

Mr. Koo studied economics at St. John's University (Shanghai, China) and did his postgraduate work at the University of Illinois, where he earned his M. S. degree. He received his A.M. and Ph.D. degrees from Harvard University.